Contents

INTRODUCTION

When I started my charity in 2004, I never realised what an impact birds would have on my life. I always thought that mammals would be my passion and whilst of course, I still love and care for sick and injured mammals, it is the birds who have taken over and it is birds that the charity now specialises in.

Rearing baby birds is one of the most enjoyable and rewarding things that I have ever learned to do. In the course of a Spring/Summer Season, I will usually rear around 250 baby birds of all types. Not bad for a small charity like ours!

Nestling Great Tits successfully hand reared and later released

Though it is a time consuming job, birds grow very quickly and once the basics of warmth and food are right, they progress with little difficulty. Giving our bird population a helping hand is vital for some species and whilst hand rearing is never as beneficial to them as being reared by their own kind, it is great to be in a position to give these beautiful creatures a second chance. This book is written specifically for those interested in taking on the job of hand rearing orphaned birds and relates to hatchling and nestling birds as these are the birds that need extra help. As most people are aware, fledglings should be left alone to continue this vital part of their development.

When I first thought about starting my "hobby" of helping wild birds, finding information was a challenge. I knew that although I had had many years of experience in the animal welfare field, it was not specialised enough to be responsible for the care of the different species I wanted to help. I spent over 12 months, prior to opening my charity, researching and learning different techniques for handling, feeding, treating injuries and accommodating animals and my husband spent many hours and thousands of pounds building my treatment room and pre-release aviaries!

I gained my information from many different sources; bought books, trawled the internet and spoke to experts and vets. Of course, over the years, I have tried new techniques, changed diets and discovered some new ideas and recipes. What some say works for them, hasn't necessarily worked for me and it is trying to replicate the natural diet in an achievable form that is most challenging and not always pleasant.

Now, this small book is the culmination of the information that I have gathered together in the last few years of rearing birds and gives as much practical advice as possible for someone interested in helping orphaned birds. I hope that this book can provide assistance to someone thinking of caring for baby birds. Birds need our help now, more than ever as they face so many more unnatural habitats fraught with man-made dangers.

Probably the most important information you will read in this book is this:- remember that you are doing this to give the bird a second chance in the wild. Resist the temptation to talk to or handle the birds, or let them become accustomed to pets. Birds, especially the Crow family and Birds of Prey can become imprinted on humans very easily. If this happens, the bird will not survive in the wild and you will have condemned him, unnecessarily, either to life in captivity or death and that is simply unforgivable.

I hope that I have provided all the information that you need to start caring for baby birds. You will find a guide at the back of the book that will provide information about where to obtain all of the items mentioned throughout the chapters and an identification guide on our website to help you determine the family that your bird belongs to. However, do feel free to email me for further advice at info@wildlife-rescue.org.uk

Samantha Bedford
Bedfordshire Wildlife Rescue

Sam with Oliver, a hand reared Barn Owl, now a resident

WILDIFE AND THE LAW

There are no specific licences required for the purposes of wildlife rehabilitation, but there is legislation that covers the keeping and releasing of rehabilitated wildlife.

The Wildlife and Countryside Act 1981

Under the Wildlife and Countryside Act 1981, subject to the provisions therein, it is an offence to take any bird from the wild. However, the following section will apply to anyone rehabilitating birds:-

Part 1, Section 4 of the Act states:-

(2) Notwithstanding anything in the provisions of section 1 or any order made under section 3, a person shall not be guilty of an offence by reason of-

(a) the taking of any wild bird if he shows that the bird had been disabled otherwise than by his unlawful act and was taken solely for the purpose of tending it and releasing it when no longer disabled;

(b) the killing of any wild bird if he shows that the bird had been so seriously disabled otherwise than by his unlawful act that there was no reasonable chance of its recovering; or

(c) any act made unlawful by those provisions if he shows that the act was the incidental result of a lawful operation and could not reasonably have been avoided.

Therefore, a person finding an injured bird can take it from the wild for the purposes of rehabilitation, or if it is too badly injured for rehabilitation, for the purposes of euthanasia.

Part 1, section 7 of the Act refers to those birds that are kept in captivity for the rest of their lives. Though this of course is not the aim of your efforts, there are occasions when wild disabled birds will settle into captivity. If that species of bird appears of Schedule 4 of the Wildlife and Countryside Act 1981, you will be required to register the bird. See Appendix 1 for a list of Schedule 4 birds.

Rehabilitators must also be aware of **Part 1, Section 14 of the Act**, which specifies:-

1) Subject to the provisions of this Part, if any person releases or allows to escape into the wild any animal which—

(a) is of a kind which is not ordinarily resident in and is not a regular visitor to Great Britain in a wild state; or

(b) is included in Part I of Schedule 9, he shall be guilty of an offence.

See appendix 1 for a list of Schedule 9 animals.

LEGISLATION - The Animal Welfare Act 2006

This Act makes owners and keepers responsible for ensuring that the welfare needs of their animals are met. When you take an animal from the wild, you become its temporary owner or keeper.

The Act requires the need:

1. For a suitable environment (place to live)

2. For a suitable diet
3. To exhibit normal behaviour patterns
4. To be housed with, or apart from, other animals (if applicable)
5. To be protected from pain, injury, suffering and disease

The Animal Welfare Act does not cover wild animals living in the wild, but does cover any wild animal taken from the wild and protected from certain acts, such as unnecessary suffering. For the purposes of the Act those animals taken into Rehabilitators are deemed "protected" by that rehabilitator and the rehabilitator must comply with the above mentioned needs.

The animals need to exhibit normal behaviour patterns will of course be compromised by the very fact that it is in some sort of confinement whilst be rehabilitated. As long as the confinement does not compromise the ability of the animal to survive upon release it should comply with this step according to the RSPCA guidelines. You must be able to justify that the confinement will ensure the animal's survival on release, i.e. confinement due to treatment of a fracture is absolutely necessary so that the fracture heals and the animal can be released back to the wild.

There is still some discussion about whether the Government is going to introduce further regulations for "sanctuaries". The definition of a "sanctuary" and what further regulations are likely has not yet been decided. The RSPCA's guidance for Wildlife Rehabilitator's is well worth reading and can be found on their website.

I would also recommend that if you start doing regular rehabilitation work that you contact your RSPCA Wildlife Officer and introduce yourself. I have worked with the RSPCA for many Years now and have always found that so long as you are doing things properly, they are so helpful. Should you become a rehabilitator for them you will need to agree to follow their guidelines but a good working relationship with the Society and with any other rehabber is beneficial to all parties and particularly the animals.

FIRST THINGS FIRST – SO YOU WANT TO HELP BIRDS?

There are two main things to consider when thinking of getting into wild bird rehabilitation:

- Time
- Money

Time

If you work full time, simply forget it, you cannot care for orphaned baby birds if you are at work. Hatchling and nestling birds need to be fed for an average of 14-15 hours per day, sometimes as frequently as every 15 minutes. It may only take 3 weeks for your bird to wean onto solid foods, but for that 3 weeks, that bird is dependent on you so if you cannot commit to its care, then you must find someone else who can.

Money

The rehabilitation of wildlife is not cheap. You will need to cover the costs of all of the food, the bird will need, plus you will need to provide other feeding equipment, heat and suitable accommodation for the bird's pre-release requirements. Add to this the costs of any veterinary charges if the bird needs medical treatment and you will soon see how expensive it can be.

Other Considerations

You must undertake the care of the bird for the right reasons. You are not rearing the bird to be a pet and must be prepared not to treat it as such. It should not be necessary to handle the bird (excepting first aid requirements) other than to weigh it or clean its bedding. Never cuddle the bird or allow it to become accustomed to pets or children. If you have a houseful of cats, dogs or children, this is not the ideal place in which to rear a bird. In order to survive the bird needs a quiet, stress free environment. This is a wild animal and it will not survive in the wild unless it avoids humans and domestic pets. Irresponsible people who imprint birds and having done this damage, then want rescue centres to care for the bird for the rest of its life or to wave a magic wand and make it wild are incredibly frustrating to those doing the job properly.

The only, rather controversial exception to this rule is in the case of a bird with a disability. Whilst I'm not a great fan of captive birds at all, I found myself in a situation in 2006 where I had to face a really tough decision. A Barn Owl who came into us as a tiny newly hatched chick was subsequently found to have a wing deformity at about 6 weeks of age and we had to decide whether to euthanase him or keep him, possibly for 20 years. I decided to keep him and have never regretted that decision though it is a big commitment to keep his life enriched and as happy as it can be.

WHY HELP BIRDS?

I have been asked in the past whether it could be said that the work carried out by wildlife "rehabbers" is interfering with nature? The theory behind this argument is based on Darwin's theory of natural selection or "survival of the fittest", ie those animals that are abandoned by their parents are the weak links in nature's chain and should therefore be left to die so that only the strongest and fittest go on to reproduce.

If it were the case that the only juvenile birds presented to rehabbers were these "weak links", then maybe these protagonists would have a point. However, it is the experience of most rehabbers that injured and orphaned wild animals have generally ended up that way, not because of any natural occurrence at all but usually through interference in their environment by humans. We have a variety of situations that lead to a baby bird being brought in to us in the orphan season. Many are brought in as a result of that age old problem of people picking up fledglings unnecessarily, numerous baby birds are abandoned after the tree, shrub or guttering that they are nesting in is cut down or removed and over 50% of our orphaned bird casualties last year were pulled out of their nests by cats, a non indigenous predator introduced to the birds' environment by humans. In reality the very fact that these birds are nesting in our man-made gardens, removes any natural element to the whole process.

Also, humans are by nature an altruistic species; quite simply it is in our nature to help others, particularly others who are weak and vulnerable. Nothing can be as weak and vulnerable as a baby, of any species, left out to die. Even Darwin acknowledged that his theory of natural selection could be fatally flawed by the concept of altruism!

Blackcap

Without a doubt, we have become a nation of bird lovers in the UK in recent decades. The amount of money spent on wild bird food these days is phenomenal and it is believed that around 3 million people go bird watching each Year. But aside from the obvious pleasure that many people derive from feeding birds, the survival of birds is actually necessary to the health of our planet. They pollinate plants, spread vital seeds, clear our gardens of damaging insects and can even control the rodent population.

Birds are also key to indicating environmental changes, Kingfishers disappeared from many of our polluted rivers and the effect of pesticides such as DDT on many different species of birds, most notably Peregrine Falcons, was found to have been devastating to the environment.

Feeding garden birds is vital for the future survival of some species and is now even believed to be having an effect on the evolution of some, notably the Blackcap. Scientists have discovered that due to the amount of food available to them via bird tables, a splinter group of Blackcaps is no longer migrating to Spain from Germany, instead preferring to spend the winter season in Britain. Over the course of 30 generations, the birds visiting Britain have evolved different-shaped wings more suited to the shorter journey to Britain and narrower beaks, more suitable to the food here. This could never have happened previously as the birds would never have survived in our winter environment prior to the existence of so many bird feeders.

It is well known that there has been a national decline in the numbers of many species of birds, and most people will remember seeing different species of birds in their garden 20 years ago to today. How many of us remember hearing a cuckoo as a child? Today the cuckoo is a red listed species of bird that has a 50% decline in its breeding population over the last 25 years. Even the humble Starling is in trouble and the sights of vast clouds of Starlings performing in the dusk sky are now a thing of the past.

In both our 2007 and 2008 orphan seasons, we reared an average of 75 Blackbirds in May and June of each Year and only 2 of its close relative, the Song Thrush, which is now also a Red Listed species. The reason for the decline of this species is down to the changes in agriculture and increased uses of pesticides and insecticides. Farming methods are unlikely to change significantly with the growth of the population and our back gardens will have to be the hope of saving species such as the Song Thrush. As our garden nature reserves do become the feeding and breeding grounds for more birds, it is inevitable that we are going to become increasingly aware of their health and welfare and as a natural progression, hopefully, take responsibility for both.

Aside from the issue of our basic instinct to nurture, the feeling of satisfaction you derive from helping a vulnerable creature is second to none. The simple fact is that birds need all the help they can get. Of course you should help any genuinely injured or orphaned bird. Far from "interfering with nature" you are simply redressing the balance of the damage that our species has caused to the natural environment.

Song Thrush, now a Red Listed Species

WHEN SHOULD YOU INTERFERE?

All baby birds fall into one of two groups, altricial and precocial (though within the precocial group, also falls the semi-precocials which will need a little extra help than their independent precocial cousins). Most garden birds are the former, though should you start caring for birds on a regular basis you will certainly find yourself caring for a precocial bird before long

ALTRICIAL

These are the birds that stay in the nest and are featherless or downy and completely dependent upon their parent for food and warmth. This covers most of your common garden birds, such as Blackbirds, Blue Tits, Robins, Starlings, Crows, Pigeons and Birds of Prey. There are two specific age groups that you MUST help if they need it, Hatchlings and Nestlings, and one age group, the Fledglings, that absolutely SHOULD be left alone.

HATCHLINGS

These are birds who have literally hatched within the last few days. They may have been blown or pushed out of the nest and can be distinguished from nestlings and fledglings by the fact that they will be featherless and unless you have got to them really quickly, they will also be cold. These birds are incredibly vulnerable and if out of the nest will always need your help.

NESTLINGS

These are older than hatchlings and tend to be most vulnerable to predation, particularly by cats. It may be because they are more vocal and so easily discovered. Nestling birds will usually only be partially feathered (generally bald under the wings) and in some cases, gape their mouths in order to receive food from their parents. They will readily gape at you and are not particularly nervous about a change in surroundings. These birds will also need your help.

Hatchling Blackbirds
– featherless and unable to move outside of the nest

Nestling Sparrow
– some feathers but unable to evade predators out of the nest

FLEDGLINGS

When organisations such as the RSPCA and the RSPB advertise their annual Spring campaigns to leave baby birds alone, a closer look will inform you that they are in fact talking about fledglings. Neither organisation would expect you to leave a truly orphaned or injured hatchling or nestling bird to die and in fact, both organisations frequently refer calls on to rescue facilities like ours. The message to leave fledglings alone is absolutely correct, but it can be difficult to recognise a fledgling if you know little about birds?

Fledgling Thrush and Robin

Fledglings are those that you are most likely to see in the garden. They will have acquired nearly all of their flight feathers and will usually have a stubby set of tail feathers as well as the last parts of the fleshy yellow corners to their mouths enabling them to gape at their parents for food. Fledglings are usually found on the ground and are able to hop, run and flutter but not properly fly. These birds should ALWAYS be left where they are, as their parents will be watching and feeding them. They are expert hiders and fledging is an integral part of their development. Fledglings are extremely nervous and will NOT readily accept food from you. The stress of being near humans is often fatal for these birds, so we will always advise people not to pick them up unless they are injured. If someone has already picked up the bird and found afterwards that it is a fledgling, they should return it to where they found it. Don't worry too much about the parents abandoning the fledgling once handled, as a birds sense of smell is not sufficient to notice.

If there is concern that the bird may be attacked by a cat, there is a simple method of safely reuniting the bird with its parents. All you need is a plastic plant pot or a cardboard box and a washing line! Take a pot/box and peg or clip it to a washing line with the opening facing outward. Pop the bird inside and within an hour or so, the bird's parents should come down to investigate.

The ideal way to return Fledgling to parent, safely!

Because the pot/box will hang naturally at an angle, the bird will not get out but the parents can get in to feed it. The bird therefore remains safe and off the ground whilst finishing fledging. However, if the parents do not come down within two hours, treat the bird as abandoned and rescue it.

If you have a rotary line you can sit a box on top of it with the opening facing outwards. Because of the shape of the line, the box will sit at a 45 degree angle, meaning that the bird cannot get out but the parents can get in. If the bird has already been injured however, it will need help and medication.

Pigeons and Collared Doves are also altricial birds but look completely different to most altricial garden birds. Both species are covered in a soft yellow down and if any of this down is still showing on the youngsters, then they are not ready to leave the nest and should be rescued.

Hatchling Pigeon

Young Collared Doves will often be found in late Winter/early Spring and though these are technically fledglings these early bred birds will tend to have a calcium deficiency meaning that they are unable to fly and sometimes, even unable to walk. These should ALWAYS be picked up.

Though Birds of Prey are altricial and therefore go through the same stages as previously mentioned, Tawny owl fledglings or owlets undergo a period of "branching" before they can fly and may be found sitting at the base of a tree.

If the owlet appears healthy and mobile it should be left to continue this part of its development. However, do check up on the bird after 24 hours. If it is still in the same place it is likely that there is a problem.

Tawny Owl Chick

PRECOCIAL

Unlike Altricial birds, these birds are independently able to move around and follow their parents to find food. Precocial species include ducklings, goslings, cygnets (swans), moorhens, coots, partridges and pheasants.

Some precocial birds can be ready to leave the nest in a very short period of time after hatching. Precocial however, does not mean that they can completely fend for themselves, most are unable to thermoregulate (control their body temperatures), and they depend on their parents to brood them with body heat for a short period of time.

There are also **Semi-precocial** birds, such as Gulls and Gamebirds, who can move around and follow their parents but must be shown and fed food and must also be brooded for warmth.

A fascinating fact about precocial birds is that their brains are larger at birth relative to their body size than an altricial bird's brain, hence the precocial birds ability to fend for itself. However, as they become adults their brains do not grow much bigger. Altricial birds, whose brains are relatively small at birth, hence their helplessness, show a much larger brain growth throughout their developmental stages and so as adults, altricial birds end up with comparatively larger brains relative to their body size than their precocial counterparts.

Lone precocial birds are totally incapable of surviving even though they may be able to find food for themselves. They are incredibly vulnerable to predators and hypothermia without their mother's protection and warmth. A lone precocial bird should be deemed abandoned and picked up; this includes ducklings, pheasant or partridge chicks, gulls, moorhens, coots and all other precocial and semi precocial birds

The Precocial chick you are most likely to see is the Mallard Duckling

EQUIPMENT FOR THE REHABILITATION AND RELEASE OF WILD BIRDS

The equipment necessary for you will depend on whether you are intending to care for just the occasional rescued bird or whether you intend to do it on a regular basis.

When I made the decision to start caring for orphaned birds, I had no equipment and certainly no birds. I have had calls from people in the past who have decided to start caring regularly for birds only after they have found their first orphan, which is really the wrong way round. You should set up first, research all of the food and release requirements of the various families of birds and any necessary first aid methods and only then, when you are sure you are ready, take in your first orphan.

Whether you decide to dedicate a room to your orphans or a whole building, it will need to be heated. I converted my garage building by insulating and cladding the walls and ceilings as well as setting up independent heaters. We have recently had to extend our facility however, as we have become known and there is so much demand for our service and we now have a dedicated nursery room just for our baby birds.

Part of our dedicated bird nursery room

Of course, you will also need cages of various sizes. Second hand cages are just fine and I trawled around charity shops, car boot sales and ebay for all of my cages when I started. I also put notices up in lots of local vets asking for carriers and still get calls today as a result.

All baby birds require a direct source of heat such as a heat lamp or heat pad in addition to the ambient heat provided in the room. Brooder lamps or cat comforter heat pads are an essential piece of equipment for anyone intending to care for baby birds.

Baby Barn Owl in "nest"

For larger birds, such as Owls I use a pet carrier with a heat pad at the bottom. The pad is covered with thick newspaper and then a towel is twisted into a ring (doughnut shape) to act as a nest and lined with kitchen paper. The baby can be monitored constantly and more newspaper added or taken away until the heat is right for that baby

For the smaller varieties of garden bird, I use enclosed plastic Zoozone cages under a brooder lamp. These are great as they act as incubators and keep the heat in on all sides. We also have dedicated brooder units from Brinsea, which are fantastic for newly hatched chicks, but are also very expensive.

For newly hatched, naked birds, the temperature of its surrounding environment needs to be about around 35° (possibly higher still for the very tiny birds such as Blue Tits which we maintain at around 37-38° initially. As the bird begins to grow feathers (or if it has down – Gulls, Birds of Prey, Pigeons) the heat can be reduced to 30° for nestlings and 25° for fledglings. These temperatures are important as you do not want your birds wasting precious energy trying to keep warm, when they should be using it for growth. Signs that the birds are not warm enough will be a reluctance to feed or move and a hunched appearance. Signs that the birds are too hot are open mouthed breathing and a stretching out, particularly of the neck. When not using a temperature controlled incubator you will need to monitor the temperature inside the nest with a thermomemeter.

A Zoozone with overhead heatlamp

I would not recommend a cardboard box to keep your baby in as it will be exposed to your heat source on a constant basis while you rear the bird and so may be a hazard. The small plastic tanks that you find in pet shops for reptiles can be good for the tiny species of bird and quite cost effective if it is likely that you will be rearing your bird as a one off. You will also need a bird cage for when the bird is too big for the tank and no longer needs the heat source, but isn't quite ready to go into an aviary.

A small plastic dish will be ideal as your makeshift nest bowl and kitchen roll will be needed to line it. I have a lovely volunteer who spends the Winter knitting me little nest pouches which are ideal, but you don't need to go that far! Margarine tubs make great nests, lined with tissue paper. Straw and Hay should never be used as bedding as they contain dust and mould spores. The dish is then placed in a newspaper lined plastic tank with the brooder lamp overhead. A thermometer inside the tank is valuable if using an overhead lamp.

However, you should also put a small dish in one corner filled with wet kitchen towels to act as a humidifier but make sure that the bird cannot fall in the dish and drown! When the bird has outgrown both the tank and the bird cage, is fully feathered and able to flutter, it is time to introduce him to an aviary environment. If you do not have an aviary, you should contact another rehabilitator and see if you can make arrangements with them. However, if you intend to rear birds on a regular basis, then at least one aviary is a must.

Again, I got my first two aviaries from ebay at exceptionally reasonable prices. In fact, the second aviary cost us nothing at all after we told the seller what it was for. He wouldn't accept payment and asked us to treat it as a donation!!

A feed station set up outside one of my smaller aviaries.

The bird will stay in the aviary for a period of 2 weeks or so to acclimatise. Most young garden birds follow their parents around and so are taught to find food. Because we are obviously not able to do this, I set up bird tables and feeding stations right outside the aviaries. The types of feeders and foods are identical to those set up inside the aviary so that the birds recognise them. This gives them an extra headstart when they're out in the big wide world.

My small charity is proof that you don't need acres of land to be able to help wildlife. My modest suburban garden is no more than one quarter of an acre but I have used what space I do have wisely. I now have 8 aviaries and a duck pen nestled amongst my trees and shrubs.

Most gardens are suitable for the release of the usual species of garden birds. However, if you want the birds to stick around, you need to have a suitable environment for them.

Bird feeders and bird baths are all very well but shrubs and trees complete the picture. I don't have anything particularly exotic in my garden, a few Common Box Shrubs, Birch Trees, Cherry Trees, Ivy, Holly and Sycamore Trees, yet I have the most amazing array of garden birds. My Sycamores have an almost constant flow of the various members of the Tit families after the aphids that swarm around it. I also make sure that the borders of my garden are not too tidy. Provide a log heap and let nettles, ground ivy and wild flowers grow and they will provide a veritable feast of insects for your birds.

Most importantly NEVER use chemicals in your garden if you want to see your birds thrive. Insecticides kill invertebrates that are then eaten, possibly by the birds that you have just spent your time hand rearing and even if they don't eat them, if you kill off all of the invertebrates, what will they eat??

The only other thing to mention here is about feeder hygiene. Whilst I fully advocate Year round feeding for garden birds, it is a fact that birds are now increasingly succumbing to various diseases as a result of poor hygiene. I am fanatical about my bird feeding areas and they are washed and disinfected with Virkon once a week all year round and left to dry out naturally. This ensure that all of the now increasingly prevalent viral, fungal, protozoal and bacterial problems are dealt with.

HYGIENE

Rearing baby animals is no different at all to rearing baby humans. Hygiene is absolutely vital if you want your babies to survive.

Your hygiene kit will include:-

- Paper Towels
- An approved veterinary disinfectant such as Virkon, Safe4 or Anigene
- Baby Wipes (sensitive non perfumed)
- Hand sanitister
- Sterilising tablets or solution

Paper Towels and Disinfectant - Your baby bird's environment will need cleaning out thoroughly once a day including their incubator, nest bowl etc, which should be cleaned with the disinfectant at the suggested % solution. This should be completely dry before the babies are returned and so you will need a spare heated area to keep them warm while you do this.

Any bedding they have (knitted nests, paper towels, etc) will need frequent changing as you won't be able to clean up each and every faecal sac they pass as they do it, but they must not be allowed to sit in faecal matter as this will cause sores.

Baby wipes are used to wipe beaks and faces free of any spilled food as

Nests and nest linings must be kept clean!

feathers must be protected and free from any detritus which could act as a breeding ground for bacteria.

Hand Sanitiser - Ideally, you should use this before handling the babies though they should not be handled unless absolutely necessary anyway.

Sterilising tablets – Everything used to feed the babies from Pastettes, syringes, crop needles, teats or feeding bowls and anything else must be sterilized once used and prior to any further use.

FEEDING EQUIPMENT

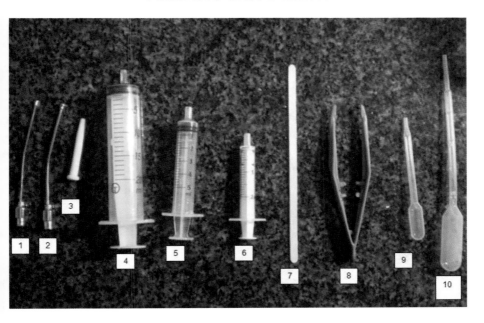

There is such a variety of equipment used for the hand rearing of baby birds. Shown above are just some of the items I could not do without.

1   Stainless steel crop tubes 18g

2   Stainless steel crop tubes 14g

3   Catac ST1 Teat (with the end cut off to make a soft feeding tube)
     Alternatively, you can also now buy flexible crop tubes.

4   20ml Syringe

5   5ml Syringe

6   2ml Syringe

7   Wooden Coffee Stirrer

8   Plastic Tweezers

9   3" Pastette

1   1ml Pastette
0

You will also need a set of scales for weighing your babies (same time each day, after a feed) to make sure they are gaining weight sufficiently

FOOD

With the exception of some Waterbirds, Birds of Prey and Pigeons/Doves, all baby birds are fed on insects by their parents. It is difficult for us humans to know which insects are good food, whether they have come into contact with toxins (or contain gut toxins in the case of earthworms), not to mention the sheer logistics of obtaining the necessary amount and variety of grubs required and so we have to find suitable alternatives.

Some people choose to use live mealworms as a diet but I personally do not consider these a good idea because a) they do not provide enough variety and b) the chitinous skins are a serious digestive concern for small chicks. Whatever alternatives we choose however, need to follow the minimum nutritional values required for good growth and feather development.

The nutritional requirements of birds are not so very different from our own, they require Protein, Fats, Carbohydrates, Minerals and Vitamins just as we do. Protein and Fat are by far the most important of these requirements so that they can grow and develop feathers. By looking at various insect nutritional values, we can begin to get a good idea of the protein/fat levels required

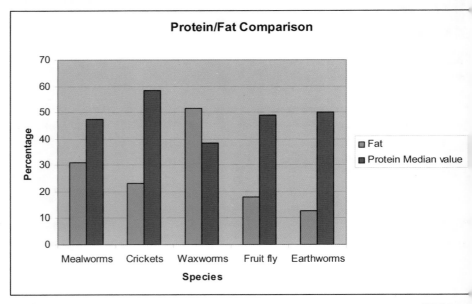

BSAVA figures

Working out an average Protein and Fat content of the 5 species together gives us the following Protein/Fat/Carbohydrate ratios needed to rear our chicks.

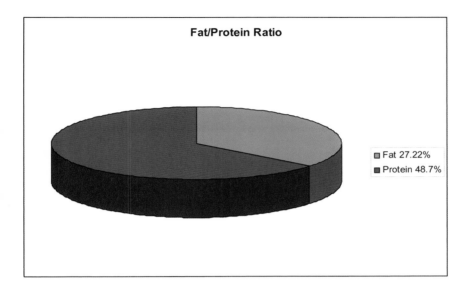

Fat/Protein Ratio

- Fat 27.22%
- Protein 48.7%

So, a diet with approximately 48% Protein, 27% Fat is what we're looking for.

I have experimented with many different food choices over the Years and only recently stopped using a corn based breeding mash for the seed eating birds such as finches (though I do still use it for Pigeons/Doves). Whilst this food seemed great for nestlings and fledglings, when used to rear finch hatchlings the protein levels were just insufficient.

I've also used tinned dog food mixed with insect food before which is a great source of protein, but it spoils so quickly. Eventually I decided to try dried dog or cat food instead but found when looking into it further, that many of the supermarket stocked dried foods contain vegetable protein rather than animal protein and this is no use at all. Brands such as Iams Kitten, Hills and particularly the brand I now favour, Applaws Kitten, all contain animal protein of around 40-48% and this is something you need to look for. I particularly like using the dried food mix because I can make up a large batch at the beginning of the season and just scoop out what I need before each feed and mix it with water to form a smooth thick paste.

I grind down the biscuits using a coffee grinder and add a dried insect mix and some of the corn based breeding mash which I think is beneficial in terms of additional vitamins and minerals. The ingredients are all dry the Protein to Fat Ratio works out very close to the necessary 48/27 Protein : Fat Ratio.

REARING MIX

– for 1kg

Applaws Kitten Dry Food -Chicken	600g
Bogena Universal Insect Food/Haiths Prosecto	200g
Tropican Rearing Mix/ or Kaytee Exact –	200g
Avipro Probiotic Powder –	1 tsp

Grind down the kitten biscuits preferably using a coffee grinder and then mix in the Bogena/Prosecto and Tropican/Kaytee plus the teaspoon of Avipro. Scoop out required amount and add water to form a thick paste

Make up a different batch for each set of orphans and refrigerate the mix between feeds. Research carried out by St Tiggywinkles has shown that feeding the mix straight from the fridge is not harmful to the bird and actually controls any bacterial growth that would flourish if the food were not refrigerated. Discard and change each pot every 3 or 4 hours, using fresh sterilised pots each time.

We make up a different batch of mix for each nest of orphans so that there is no cross contamination. All of the mixes are refrigerated between feeds. We use small pots so that fresh mix is made up more regularly and each pot is sterilised after use and before the next batch.

If you do not have a coffee bean grinder handy to grind the ingredients up, you can soak the biscuits in water until they are soft and then mix in the rest of the ingredients but you will need to make a fresh batch at least 4 times daily.

FIRST AID – The Basics

When your baby bird is found or is brought in to you it is likely to be suffering from shock, hypothermia, dehydration and malnourishment, so the last thing that you should do is to start filling it up with food or fluids.

Step 1: Stabilising Temperature

It is vital that baby birds are the right temperature. Too hot or too cold and they will simply not survive. They are unable to regulate their own temperature and rely entirely on their mothers for warmth. As you

Stabilising the temperature of a Dunnock chick

are now their "mother" it is your job to keep them warm.

If they are small species, unfeathered or partially feathered (and you don't have access to an incubator or brooder) the bird can be held in a loose fist to stabilise their temperature. Older, fully feathered or bigger species of birds will not need this and can be put straight into a makeshift nest with the relevant heat source. **Do not attempt to feed the baby birds or give them fluids before they are warm as this is likely to kill them.**

Once the bird feels warmer than your hand (bird's body temperature is slightly higher than ours), it can then be transferred into the makeshift nest inside the tank, under the heat lamp and the temperature of the baby monitored continuously throughout the next couple of hours to make sure it does not increase or decrease too much.

Step 2 - Rehydration

Giving fluids to birds is not particularly easy if you are inexperienced, and without veterinary assistance the only real way to administer it is orally. If the fluids enter the trachea (windpipe), the bird will die and so the method usually used to administer fluids to a bird is called gavage, though ideally you want someone with experience to show you this method, ie a vet or rehabilitator. If the bird is alert and gaping however, you should mix some rehydration fluid with the food and this will suffice. Birds of Prey will certainly benefit from having their food dipped in rehydration fluid before being fed. With very small birds, gavage is difficult but a cotton bud dipped in water and wiped along the beak will provide some moisture.

To gavage a bird, you will need a suitably sized syringe and gavage tube. For birds such as Pigeons and Doves, I use a catac ST1 teat with the end cut off. For smaller birds, you can buy specialist crop feeding tubes which are made of stainless steel and come in various sizes. The 18 gauge tube is suitable for tiny birds and the sizes increase to 16 gauge for Finch sized birds, 14 gauge for Blackbirds, 12 gauge for Wood Pigeon sized, and 8 gauge which would be suitable for very large birds such as Buzzards and Kites. There are also now flexible crop tubes made by Vetark which come in two sizes, small and large. The small size would be suitable for Blackbird sized birds and the larger is suitable for fitting on a 60ml syringe and could be used for Owls.

To estimate the amount of fluids needed you will need to weigh the bird. You can generally estimate that the bird will be between 5% and 10% dehydrated. If the bird has sunken eyes or bare skin that seems wrinkled and loose it is safe to say that it is severely dehydrated (ie 10%).

Your calculation will be :-   Estimated dehydration (%) x body weight (g) = fluid deficit (ml).
So for example a 20g bird with moderate dehydration of 7% would be calculated as 0.07 x 20 = 1.4ml.
You then also need to add on a daily maintenance fluid level of around 5% of the bodyweight.

So for our 20g bird that would be a further 1ml per day. Half of the fluid deficit amount plus the daily maintenance level should be given over the first 24 hours, ie 1.7ml for our 20g bird. You then need to give the bird the fluids in little doses not exceeding 10ml/kg. So again using our 20g bird as an example, you would give it no more than 0.2mls per feed and give it every 2 hours. There is a fluid calculation chart in Appendix 5.

The rehydration fluid must be body temperature, which for birds is 40°. If it is too cold the fluid will simply make the shock worse and of course, it is too hot, you will scald the bird. The use of Brandy and Milk are a myth. Never, ever give these fluids to a bird as they are likely to kill it.

REHYDRATION FLUID

- one level teaspoon of salt
- eight level teaspoons of sugar
- one litre of clean drinking or cooled boiled water
- Mix until dissolved

You can also purchase sachets of rehydration fluid from your veterinary practice.

Gavaging method:-

Place the bird in front of you on a towel facing you. You should try out the tube before starting the gavaging procedure to make sure that it fits well onto the syringe and contains no blockages. If the teat becomes separated from the syringe during the procedure, the bird is likely to swallow the tube and will need to be removed surgically by a vet.

Gently take hold of the head of the bird (you will need a second person to hold the bird until you become experienced). With your

Glottis

spare hand gently open the beak. Take the syringe with attached tube and make sure that you put the feeding tube into the beak on the bird's left side (your right hand side). Slide the tube over the tongue and down the throat into the crop. Do not force the tube as you may cause a rupture. The tube should just slide down into the crop of the bird. You will be able to see the Glottis (entrance to the trachea/windpipe) at the back of the tongue. Make sure none of the fluids enter the trachea. Slowly depress the syringe and administer a small amount of fluid. If the bird regurgitates, stop immediately and remove the tube. Allow the bird to calm down and start again.

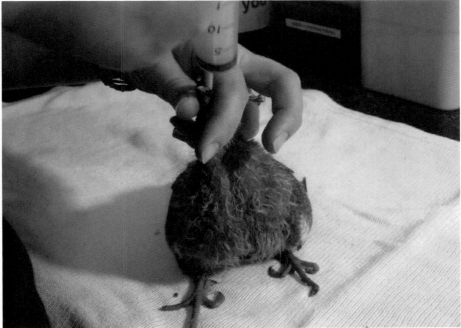
Gavaging a juvenile Pigeon

Step 3: Food

Once the previous two steps have been carried out and the bird has stabilised, you can begin to think about feeding your baby bird. You will aim to feed your bird around 10-20% of its bodyweight per day.

The bird may be reluctant to feed initially as it will not recognise that you are trying to feed it and may already be very weak. You can gently prise open the beak and put the food to the back of the throat to stimulate the bird to feed. Find out what feeding method is appropriate for your baby bird in the following chapters.

Step 4: Parasites

Your baby bird, if it is featherless is unlikely to have any parasites, but any older baby bird with feathers, particularly if already weakened is likely to have some infestation. The likely parasites will be:-

Mites/Lice – small insects that will be apparent between feathers. I use a pyrethrum based spray or powder (Johnson's Ridmite) which is safe for the bird.

Ticks – tiny grey or white pips that are attached to the skin, sucking blood. Specialist tick remover hooks are available from most pet stores. Do not use oil or just pull the tick off, or the head which is lodged under the skin of the bird will remain there and cause toxins to flood into the bird.

Flat flies – looks like a normal fly but with a flattened body and gripping feet. Without a doubt these are the bird carer's worst nightmare. They will usually be found lodged under feathers and will move when disturbed, often crawling onto the nearest warm skin. They are impossible to squash and I use a pyrethrum based spray to get rid of these too. These are usually found on the bigger birds, Wood Pigeons and Birds of Prey seem to be particular favourites.

Tick   Flat Fly   Mite

FIRST AID - Dealing With Injuries

It is inevitable that some of the birds that you have in will be injured. Baby birds that have fallen from the nest are incredibly vulnerable to danger. I have tried to cover the most common injuries that I see in baby birds each season.

Shock

No matter what has happened to the bird, there is likely to be an element of shock. An animal in shock loses body heat and fluids, its cells close down and it will die if action is not taken.

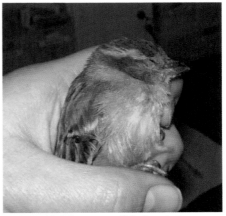

A bird in shock will be fluffed up, may have its eyes closed and will appear to be barely conscious. This is when warmth and rehydration fluids are the only recourse (see previous chapter). The bird will need to be either warmed up in the hand or placed in a makeshift nest (to keep it upright) under a heat lamp.

Make sure the bird is warm before attempting to administer fluids.

A fledgling sparrow suffering from shock

Keep noise to a minimum around the bird as this will help it recover more quickly. The possibility of shock is the reason that welfare organisations are so adamant that fledglings must be left alone. Older fledglings react very badly to being picked up by humans and will go into shock and die within a very short period of time. A drop of Bach's Rescue Remedy in the gavage fluid may also help.

Head Trauma

This can be as a result of the fall from the nest or from hitting a window whilst trying to fly. The symptoms and treatment is much the same as for shock, ie warmth and fluids. I would also in this case administer a drop of Metacam to the bird, which is a Non-Steroidal Anti-Inflammatory Drug available from vets as this will prevent any swelling of the brain and organs.

There is a limit to what the inexperienced carer can do in this situation without the assistance of veterinary drugs, so, if the bird is bleeding from the beak or has any other signs of swelling or dilated pupils, you should also speak to a sympathetic vet.

Cat Attacks

The most likely injury will be cat attack injuries, which if left untreated, will cause the bird to die of septicaemia within a couple of days. Cleaning of any injuries is very important. I use diluted Hibiscrub to clean wounds but you can also make up a saline solution by mixing 300ml of cooled boiled water with half a teaspoon of salt and clean the wounds using cotton wool.

Even the tiniest scratch from a cat's teeth will cause septicaemia due to the coating of bacteria that cats carry in their mouths. So when I am told that bird has been brought in by a cat, even if I am unable to find

evidence of injury, I will always clean the wound with diluted hibiscrub and give the bird covering antibiotics. I use a couple of different antibiotics depending on whether the wound is superficial or not but to be honest, the one drug that will always work on cat bites is amoxicillin/clavulanic acid (Synulox, Noroclav, Clavamox) administered at a dose of 35mg/kg IM (150mg/kg orally).

When giving an injection to a bird, you must hold the bird towards you and the injection is given into the breast muscle. You will need a vet in these circumstances.

Even a small cat bite like this would go septic if left

You will occasionally find that an air bubble will appear under the skin of the bird after a cat attack. This will likely be as a result of a build up of air under the skin as a result of trauma or rupture in one of the airsacs of the bird. A sterile needle from a veterinarian can be used to release the air, but the bird should be given covering antibiotics.

Fractures

Any hanging leg or wing, swelling or inability to use the leg or wing should really be checked over by a vet. Splints for leg fractures can be made from coffee stirrers or thin cardboard such as a gift card or cereal box. For the fracture of the upper leg bone (femur) of the blackbird shown here, I was able to align the fracture, which was a clean break, secure it with surgical tape, splint it with thin card and wrap the splint with co-flex bandage. The bird was able to put weight on the leg within a few days and made a full recovery.

Juvenile Blackbird with a fractured femur

Poisoning

We had a situation last Summer where both the parents of five beautiful Great Tits had been found dead the day after the homeowner had sprayed the garden with Insecticide. We had to cut the babies out of the secure nest box that the homeowner had lovingly provided in order to try and save them. Needless to say the person was distraught. Luckily, it would seem that the parents had not had time to unwittingly fill the stomachs of their offspring with the poisoned grubs and we were able to give the birds a small solution of activated charcoal solution to absorb any toxins and give them regular fluids. Luckily all of the birds survived.

Disease

There can be many different types of disease that affect garden birds but, certainly with the smaller birds, they will tend to succumb to such illness before they are ever presented to a rehabber for treatment. Some of those you may be presented with are as follows:-

Papillomavirus

Seen in Chaffinches, this virus causes growths to appear on one or both of the legs. Generally the claws of the foot affected are also overgrown and the foot can even drop off. The bird is usually presented when it can no longer walk properly or is suffering secdary problems. There have been improvements in the condition of birds who have come into care over a period of time. This being a virus there is no treatment for the actual growths but supportive care and treatment of any secondary

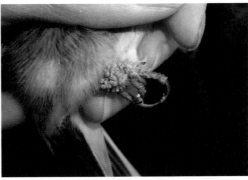

Chaffinch with Papillomavirus in the care of Totnes Birdcare

infections or other issues may help the bird overcome the virus with time. This disease should not be confused with "tassel foot" which appears very similar but is caused by mites and is treatable with Ivermectin. A vet's opinion should therefore be sought to determine which ailment is the cause.

Avian Pox

This disease is also caused by a virus which presents with pox-like lesions on the face and legs. These lesions are often infected and that infection should be treated with antibiotics. The virus will run its course eventually and the lesions will recede. Supportive treatment including tube feeding if necessary can often lead to full recovery.

Salmonellosis

Many different types of birds can be affected by salmonellosis and will tend to be emaciated, lethargic and "fluffed-up" with little or no other symptoms except possibly diarrhoea. A course of broad spectrum antibiotic such as enrofloxacin or marbofloxacin at the avian dose rate (see your vet) should assist recovery. This is of those diseases which is becoming more frequent due to a lack of bird feeder hygiene sadly.

Trichomoniasis

Many juvenile pigeons, collared doves and sometimes even Birds of Prey will come in with a condition called Trichomoniasis, also known as canker or frounce. Caused by a flagellate protozoan, the infection causes cheesy looking growths in the back of the bird's throat. Eventually, the growths become so numerous that they cover the throat entirely meaning that the bird is unable to swallow food and slowly starves to death.

The treatment for the condition is with Carnidazole (Harkers Spartrix), Ronidazole (Harkanker) or Metronidazole (Flagyl) but the medication will need to be administered carefully into the crop by gavage. If dislodged, the growths can bleed profusely and cause the bird's death, so if you are not used to handling birds, please ask a vet or experienced rehabber for help. Generally, the birds make an excellent recovery but sometimes the condition is so severe by the time the bird is brought in that it is impossible to gain access to the crop and in those situations the bird should be euthanased to prevent further suffering.

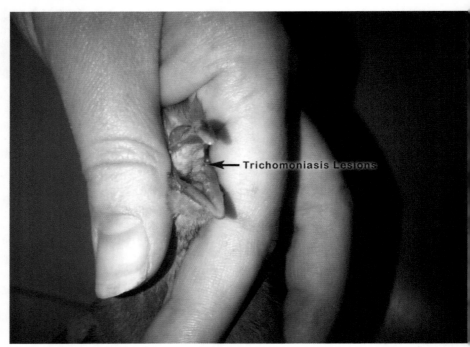

← Trichomoniasis Lesions

REARING GARDEN BIRDS – Insect Eaters

Likely species that you will see

BLACKBIRD *(Turdus merula)*	SWALLOW *(Hirundo rustica)*
BLACKCAP *(Sylvia atricapilla)*	TIT FAMILY *(Paridae Family)*
DUNNOCK *(Prunella modularis)*	THRUSHES *(Turdidae Family)*
GOLDCREST *(Regulus regulus)*	WAGTAILS *(Motacillidae Family)*
HOUSE MARTIN *(Delichon urbica)*	WARBLERS *(Sylviidae Family)*
ROBIN *(Erithacus rubecula)*	WOODPECKER *(Picidae Family)*
STARLING *(Sturnus vulgaris)*	WREN *(Troglodytes troglodytes)*

Blue Tit Nestling

The young of all of these species will require an additional source of heat; (see the Chapter; Equipment for the Rehabilitation and Release of Wild Birds). You will also need to follow the steps on basic first aid for these birds, when they arrive as they are likely to be cold and weak.

Once the bird is stabilised and ready for feeding, use a coffee stirrer or cut down 1ml pastette (use 3" Pastettes or blunted cocktail sticks for the smaller birds, such as blue tits), to simply scoop/suck up a dollop of the rearing mix and put it to the back of the baby's mouth as it gapes (about a pea sized dollop for a baby blackbird, repeated if necessary). If the baby does not gape, you can tap the side of the beak or very gently open the beak and pop the food inside. The bird will soon get the hang of it and begin to gape. A different utensil should be used for each group of babies and discarded or sterilised after each feed. The bird should always produce a dropping in a self contained sac after each feed and this must be removed. You will know if the consistency of the food is right by the condition of the faecal sac, if the food is too runny, the sac will break easily.

Feed every 20-30 mins from 7am to 9pm until weaned for Blackbird and Starling sized birds. The smaller the species, the more frequent the feeds, so Robins, Dunnocks and especially the Tit family will need feeding every 15 minutes and for longer, ie 7am to 10pm.

Faecal Sac

Do not allow the birds to become messy. Any spilled food must be wiped from the bird's face and feathers after each feed as it is a breeding ground for bacteria. The crop (located at the side of the neck) will inflate with each feed and the feed is done when the crop is full but not stretched.

Weaning

Insect eating birds should obviously wean onto insects and I usually start the weaning process by alternating the feeds between rearing mix at one feed and chopped maggots at the next. Make sure that the maggots are "clean" (ie starved in the fridge for 48 hours until the toxic black line down the centre of them has disappeared).

When the birds are able to perch in a cage, I put bowls of Prosecto or Bogena Universal Insect food and live foods such as maggots into the cage. Put the maggots into a deep sided dish so that they cannot get out (for smaller birds such as tits, the maggots should be cut up as they can find it hard to digest the tough skin). Once the birds show an interest in the weaning foods, you can begin to gradually stretch out the length of time between feeds.

You should also provide a bowl of clean fresh drinking water at this stage, though you my have to change it regularly as blackbirds and starlings especially love to bathe!

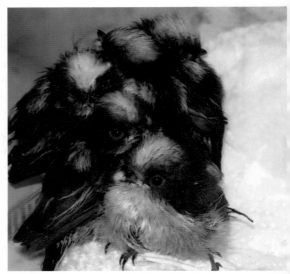
Long Tailed Tit Fledglings

When you are sure that the birds are feeding themselves, bathing and preening, able to get up and down from perches with ease, you can think about moving them into a pre-release aviary. Whilst, larger Blackbirds, Starlings and Thrushes will be ok, some of the smaller species are very delicate and so just putting them all out into an aviary and leaving them is likely to kill them. I tend to take them outside in the cage that they are in and leave it in the aviary for an hour or so to start with and bring them back in. Gradually increase the time over 2 days and then leave them in the cage with the hatch open so that they can come in and out as they please into the aviary. It goes without saying that you cannot put the tiny Tit species in the same aviary as the larger Starlings, etc as they will be unlikely to be able to get to the food. The rule of thumb is "like with like" so Blackbirds and Starlings can go together, Blue Tits and Great Tits are generally fine together, Robins and Wagtails, etc etc. If you have seed eaters as well, those same sized birds can also go together, so Goldfinches will be fine with Blue Tits and Robins but not with the larger Blackbirds, etc.

The food inside the aviary should be the same as that they have been weaned onto, so maggots and insect food. You can start to add other feeds such as crushed fatballs, chopped peanuts, etc too but set up an identical feeding station outside the aviary before you release your birds so that they can find food they recognise whilst outside.

Once they are comfortable in the aviary, they should stay there for at least 2 weeks to acclimatise to the weather and surroundings. Release early in the morning on a clear, sunny day and leave the aviary hatch open (you can make a simple hatch by cutting a panel out of the wire mesh and re-attaching the cut out with cable ties to make a flap that can be propped open) so that they can return when required (some will and some won't). Make sure that the area you are releasing them into has suitable habitat and food sources.

Great Tit Fledglings

GARDEN BIRDS: INSECT EATERS – Case Study

Of all the baby birds we see in a Summer season, the Blackbird is the most regular "orphan" brought in to us. We can rear around 70 - 80 Blackbirds in just one season.

Two of the youngest we've had were brought into us last Year, just after they had hatched. Both babies had been found lying on the ground with no sign of the nest around. One of the birds had a slight injury to its back and both were cold.

The two babies, a few days after arrival

As is always the case, the birds were held in a loose fist to raise their temperature. Both were having difficulty breathing, usually a sign of hypothermia, and this breathing difficulty eased as the birds began to warm up.

After 15–20 minutes in the hand, the birds were transferred to ready warmed nest bowls, in a zoozone tank under a heat lamp. The temperature was at 35° and the birds were weighed and each gavaged rehydration fluids then left for 10 minutes to recover. In the meantime, the rearing mix was made up. Another amount of rehydration fluids was made after an hour and the birds were given their first amount of food soon after.

Because the birds were so weak, it was necessary to gently open their beaks and using a wooden coffee

stirrer, place a pea sized amount of food at the back of the throat. Each bird was able to swallow the food and this was repeated every 30 minutes for the next 2 hours. Neither produced a faecal sac for the first 3 or 4 feeds. Thereafter, the birds had regained some strength and were able to gape for food and produce faecal sacs for removal.

Over the next week, each of the birds grew stronger and began to develop feathers.

At 2½ weeks old

From hatching to fledging takes just 3 weeks with Blackbirds and so they were soon ready to be moved into a larger cage and introduced to their weaning foods whilst still taking hand feeds. Both of the birds showed an interest in the cleaned maggots and were keen to attempt picking them up. They also both jumped straight into the bowl of water provided for them. The interest in the Universal Insect food followed soon after, though both were reluctant to give up their hand feeds.

Within another 10 days, both birds were readily taking food from dishes provided and were no longer interested in hand feeds and were ready to go our into an aviary. I have always found that if not wormed at this stage before going out to an aviary, Blackbirds and Starlings will soon begin to "sneeze" a lot (a symptom of worms) and it is much harder to catch them when they are outside. Pigeon wormers are fine for this at the recommended dose or Panacur 2.5% solution at a dose of 20mg/kg for 3 days.

Both birds settled in quickly and were soon digging around in the bark chips on the floor looking for the dried mealworms that had been left there. Both were also seen playing in the bird bath and feeding from bowls as well as flying to and from perches.

After 2 weeks in the aviary, we decided to release the birds. A small bird table was set up outside the aviary hatch and their regular food was put there first thing in the morning with the hatch lifted. Both birds took an immediate interest in the bird table and left the aviary.

Neither bird returned to the aviary, though both birds stayed in the local area and continued to visit their feed station.

Fledging and ready to go outside

GARDEN BIRDS: INSECT EATERS – Case Study 2

Every now and then, a bird arrives that is so young that we just cannot identify it immediately. We tend to call these tiny naked birds "Jellybeans".

One of these birds arrived at the end of May when we were already up to our eyes in orphans and we knew that it was going to be a hard slog for her to survive. However, she had been picked up fairly quickly, had no injuries and was already gaping for food, so we just had to try our best.

The bird was placed in our incubator which was set at 37° because she was so small an a tiny applet of

The Jellybean bird about 3 days after arrival.

water was placed in the incubator with her to act as a humidifier. She was started off, as always, with rehydration fluid mixed in with her rearing mix and we used a very fine pipette to carefully feed her every 10 minutes from 7am to 10pm. The food mix was gradually thickened over the course of a couple of hours and anyone feeding her had to make sure that no food was spilled on her and that only tiny drops were fed to her so as not to flood her mouth.

At 3 weeks old

Over the course of the next few days the tiny bird became stronger and stronger, stretching up to get her food. As she began to develop feathers we were able to identify her as a beautiful Great Tit! As she grew, feeds were reduced to every 20 minutes from 7am to 10pm

Still known as "The Jellybean" the bird continued to thrive with 20 minute feeds and we were all very proud on the day she pecked at her rearing mix herself. From there on we introduced "cleaned" Maggots and also crushed fatballs.

She was soon moved outside to our smallest aviary with a group of Blue Tits who had been reared with her. This move was, as is always the case with small birds carried out very gradually over the course of 48 hours (putting their cage in the aviary and bringing it in a night to prepare them before releasing into the aviary) and an identical food station was set up inside and outside the aviary so that the food could be easily recognised. After 2 weeks the hatch was opened and the birds were allowed out into the big wide World! None of them returned to the aviary though were seen at the feeding station the following morning.

The first time the bird fed herself

REARING GARDEN BIRDS – SEED EATERS

Likely species that you will see

BULLFINCH (Pyrrhula pyrrhula)

CHAFFINCH (Fringilla coelebs)

GREENFICH (Carduelis carduelis)

GOLDFINCH (Carduelis chloris)

HAWFINCH (Coccothraustes coccothraustes)

LINNET (Carduelis cannabina)

SISKIN (Carduelis spinus)

SPARROWS (Passeridae)

Though these birds will grow up to be seed eaters, they are also fed on the Rearing Mix. (See, Food and Feeding Equipment)

Because they are generally the finch type birds and are small, they are maintained at a heat of 35° for tinies gradually reduced to 30° and subsequently 25° when fully featherd. Using 3" mini pastettes with the end cut off is a quick and clean way of feeding. A different utensil should be used for each nest of babies and you can simply scoop or suck up some of the mix and

Full crop

Goldfinches

gently put it to the back of the throat as the bird gapes. If the bird does not gape, very gently open the beak and put the food in, the bird will soon get the hang of it. As with insect eating birds, the crop should be full (as you can see in the picture above right) but not stretched. New or sterilised Pastettes should be used for each new feed.

Greenfinch

All of the seed eating garden birds are small birds and will need feeding every 20 minutes from 7am to 10pm.

These birds will also back up to the edge of the "nest" and produce a dropping which must be removed after each feed. You will know if the consistency of the mix is right if the faecal sac can be removed in one piece without breaking.

The mix should not be allowed to become stuck to the birds' faces and feathers as this will be a breeding ground for bacteria.

Weaning

Seed eaters are weaned, when almost fully feathered by putting small dish of their rearing mix in the cage. I also find that putting the rearing mix on a teaspoon and securing the teaspoon to a branch gains a lot of interest. In addition to the rearing mix, a finch mix and niger seed should also be available as these are small enough to be picked up. Sprinkle some seeds on the floor of the cage whilst still hand feeding in order to encourage them to peck.

Once fully weaned, the birds must go into an aviary or similar environment for 2 weeks to acclimatise before they can be soft released into a suitable garden. As with the smaller Insect eaters in the previous section, this transfer to the aviary environment should be carried out very slowly.

Goldfinches

GARDEN BIRDS: SEED EATERS – Case Study

During May, we had a call about 2 baby birds that had been found sitting on a path at the bottom of a garden. They had very little feathers and the nest had been found nearby lying on the floor. There had been very strong winds the previous evening and it is likely that the nest had been blown out of the tree and both birds, about a week away from fledging were able to get out but not move far away.

Our Juvenile Chaffinch

When the two baby birds arrived, they had already been warmed up on a hot water bottle wrapped in a towel and so we were able to give them fluids immediately. Both birds gaped for food and so the rehydration fluid was mixed with the rearing mix to make it slightly more watery and both birds were fed using a 3" mini pastette with a fine tip.

Both of the birds were put into an incubator tank under a heat lamp at around 28° and were given a makeshift nest. The both accepted feeds from us without any fuss and were within a couple of hours, moved on to the usual consistency of rearing mix. As they were older birds, they were fed every half hour from 7am to 9pm.

Showing interest in a bowl of rearing mix

Within a week the birds had grown lots of feathers and were jumping about the incubator tank looking for a way out. The birds were moved into a bird cage with a small dish of their rearing mix and a few finch seeds scattered on the floor. Both jumped up onto the perches and began to explore their new environment but still called for food every half hour.

Over the next week as the birds began to peck at their dish of rearing mix, their hand feeds were reduced to every hour until they no longer accepted feeds from us at all. At this stage, it was decided that the birds were ready to be moved into an aviary. Because this species is one of the smaller "delicate" species. Their cage was lifted outside and into a small aviary for just a two hour period on a warm morning and then brought back in again. The following day the same was done and the birds were gradually left out for longer each day over a few days and brought back in at night.

On a particularly warm day, the birds were let out of the cage and into the aviary to fly about. This was the first night they were left outside.

When we checked the following morning both birds were fine, tucked up in the topmost corner of the aviary and so over the course of the next week, their food dishes were gradually removed and replaced with bird feeders filled with wild bird seed and sunflower hearts which they would recognise around the garden when released.

The birds were left in the aviary for two weeks then released via an aviary hatch first thing one morning. Both returned to the aviary for food later in the day but soon found the other feeders around the garden and left the aviary for good.

Ready to go outside

REARING GARDEN BIRDS – Crop Feeders

Likely species that you will see

FERAL PIGEON (*Columba livia*)

WOOD PIGEON (*Columba palumbus*)

COLLARED DOVE (*Streptopelia decaocto*)

STOCK DOVE (*Columba oenas*)

These birds can be fed using Tropican Breeding Mash or Kaytee Exact Handrearing Formula up to the consistency of double cream. The method of feeding is via gavage and you will need a 2ml, 10ml and 20ml syringe together with a Catac ST1 teat (with the tip cut off) for each bird.

On arrival, the bird should be warmed up either by holding in a loose fist or in a suitable incubator environment set to around 30°-35°. Once warm they should be given just rehydrating fluids (see First Aid). If the bird has gone without food for any length of time and you then fill the crop up, the bird is likely to develop a condition called sour crop. Over-filling the crop can also cause this condition, so be sure to start off the feeding with just rehydration fluids for the first feed and then gradually introduce the food mix into the fluid at the ratio of ¼ Tropican to ¾ water, then half and half at the next feed, then ¾ Tropican to ¼ water and finally Tropican only. The volume of fluid given will depend on the age of the bird, but guides are below:-

Feeding Guide:-   (lower amounts are for collared doves)

Hatchlings   *still completely covered in yellow down*
Newly hatched birds will require a runnier mixture for the first week (consistency of milk). Feed **1 -2 mls every 2 hours from 7am to 8pm**

Squeakers   *Downy with some feathers coming through*
Feed 5 to 10mls every 3 hours from 7am to 8pm

Squabs   *Mostly feathered with some yellow down still visible around neck and on head*
Feed 15 to 20mls every 4 hours (wood pigeons may need an extra 5 - 10 mls)

Use a clean syringe and tube for each bird. After feeding, wash the tube and syringe well in hot, soapy water; rinse and place in sterilising solution.

Wood Pigeons from left to right Hatchling, Squeaker and Squab

Weaning:-

When the bird reaches the squab stage you can begin to introduce small seeds, such as budgie mix for the birds to practice picking up. They will still need normal feeds until you are sure they are eating. Gradually swap the budgie seed for a wild bird seed mix. Once weaned, the birds must go into an aviary or similar environment for 2 weeks before they can be released into a suitable garden.

Sour Crop:-

This is basically where there is an overload of bacteria in the crop causing it to cease working. Whatever is in the crop is therefore not digested and will ferment in the crop eventually killing the bird. In order to prevent the condition sterilise the feeding tube after each feed and always use a separate clean tube for each bird. Check the crop in between each feed (located above the birds chest and below the neck) to make sure it is empty. If the crop still feels like an inflated balloon when you come to feed it again, it may be that the bird has sour crop. The crop must be expressed to remove the contents (you may need help from a vet to do this) but it basically involves inverting the bird and massaging the contents of the crop back up the oesophagus and out through the mouth. You will immediately be able to smell the sour smell of sour crop and the treatment to cure the condition (as long as it has not progressed too far) is as follows:-

- Remove Contents of Crop
- Flush crop with saline
- Re-introduce rehydration fluids then gradually back to solids over 24 hours.

Calcium Deficiency

Young Collared Doves found in March/April tend to have left the nest and be found sitting on the floor unable to fly and sometimes even unable to walk. The reason for their predicament is a chronic calcium deficiency believed to be brought about by the fact that they nest too early and lack good quality food and vitamin D to nourish their chicks sufficiently. Feeding them on formula with an added drop of liquid calcium tends to be enough to boost this deficiency but if their feet or limbs are bent you will need to seek assistance from an experienced carer to splint them.

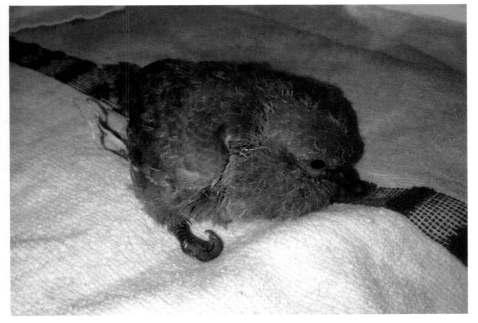

2 week old Dove with calcium deficiency

GARDEN BIRDS: Crop Feeders – Case Study

Aside from Blackbirds, Wood Pigeons are our most numerous patients. One of the many "Woodies" brought in to us was a newly hatched one, who had fallen out of his nest. It has to be said that pigeons do not make particularly good nests in the first place. They tend to find a nice crossed over set of branches, place a few twigs in a haphazard fashion and then lay some eggs!! They usually lay 2 eggs in a nest and the male bird will sit on them during the day and the female at night.

The baby bird had been found after being brought into the house by a cat and had a small injury to one of his legs. He was also cold and lethargic. The bird was held in a loose fist for almost an hour before he began to warm up and become more alert. His injury was cleaned with a dilute hibiscrub and a cotton bud and he was given an injection of Amoxycare LA to prevent infection.

Once warm, we were able to give the bird Rehydration fluid and transfer him into a nest bowl in an incubator tank under a heat lamp at around 30°. The bird was left for an hour and then given 2 mls of diluted Tropican via gavage. The crop was checked after a further 2 hours to make sure that it was functioning properly and the bird was fed again with a further 2 mls of the runny mixture. Over the next few days, the mix of Tropican was gradually thickened until it was the consistency of double cream and the bird progressed well on feeds every 2 hours from 7am to 8pm. The bird was soon joined by two other orphaned Wood Pigeons.

After 2 weeks of feeds gradually increasing feeds from 2 to 4 hourly, the bird had grown a good set of feathers, though his yellow baby down was still evident. At the first sight of the feathers, the bird had been moved from the incubator into a cage with a nest bowl. As the bird showed signs of being able to perch on the edge of the bowl, he was also given a free standing perch to use.

At the age of 4 weeks, the bird was taking 30 mls of food every 4 hours and was also given a small dish of budgie seeds to practice picking up by himself. Once able to pick up the small seeds a larger bird seed mix was mixed in and the bird was moved into an aviary. By this time, we had 6 other juvenile Wood pigeons and the pigeons

were all put together. After a further 2 weeks in the aviary the birds were all eating and flying well. We decided that the birds were ready to go and a bird table was set up outside the aviary hatch. The hatch was then left open first thing on the following morning and the birds slowly made their way outside. All of the birds continued to visit the bird table for 2 to 3 weeks following their release and all are still making occasional visits.

The pigeon, fully grown and ready to go into an aviary

REARING CORVIDS

Likely species that you will see

CROW (*Corvus corone*)   RAVEN (Corvus corax)
JACKDAW (*Corvus monedula*)   ROOK (Corvus frugilegus)
JAY (*Garrulus glandarius*)
MAGPIE (*Pica pica*)

Juvenile Magpie

All of these birds can be started off on the rearing mix (See Food and Feeding Equipment) but obviously, the amount given needs to be in larger quantities than for the insect eaters, a marble sized portion for magpies and jackdaws will suffice and larger still for Rooks and Crows. Use either plastic tweezers or lollipop sticks to feed. **These birds should be fed every 30 minutes from 7am to 9pm.**

As they grow bigger and start to develop feathers it is necessary to introduce fur and feather to their diet. This is not a particularly pleasant job for anyone who loves birds, but these Corvids, like Birds of Prey need this fur or feather in order to develop properly. Obviously, it is not possible to offer them their natural diet and so we use day old hatchery cockerel chicks which are the only alternative. It definitely takes some getting used to, especially as you must chop up the chicks (I find it easier to cut them up with a pair of kitchen scissors reserved for the purpose). However, as unpleasant as it is, the chicks are cockerels and so killed as surplus to requirements in the farming industry. You may as well make sure they're used for a good purpose!

Do not give young corvids the egg sac, head or feet of the chick as these may cause damage to your growing bird. These birds are incredibly messy and will need their nests cleaning throughout the day, probably at every other feed.

Weaning:-

Corvids, when fully feathered and able to stand can be weaned onto chopped up chicks (without added rearing mix), mashed up dog food, soaked kitten biscuits and Bogena Universal Insect food

Nestling Crow

with a pinch of SA37 Vitamin powder. They also enjoy cheese, cooked pasta and potatoes.

As with all other birds, these birds will need 2 weeks in an aviary environment to make sure they can fly before being soft released into a suitable garden.

There is a serious warning to be had with rearing these types of birds. They are hugely entertaining, intelligent and very, very cute. You **MUST** resist the temptation to interact with these particular species as they are highly intelligent and are the easiest family of birds to tame. If you do tame them, you will be left with a bird that cannot be released back to the wild as it will be unable to mix with its own kind and will choose to interact with humans. This will likely lead to it being shot or trapped and killed.

Feather Damage in Corvids

We often see juvenile crows with white patchy feathers. These are as a result of poor diet and when severe, are very brittle, leaving the bird unable to fly properly. In these cases the bird will have to moult a whole set of new feathers which can take up to a year in an aviary.

Being fed on Chopped chicks and soaked kitten biscuits sprinkled with SA37 will help the new feathers to grow in an aviary environment but where it is severe, this process could take a Year or more.

A fellow rehabber, Lucy Kells, at The Wildlife Aid Foundation has recently had some success with imping Corvid feathers, which involves attaching donor feathers to replace the damaged ones which if fully successful would reduce captivity time significantly.

Juvenile Crow with severely damaged feathers

CORVIDS: - Case Study

Any volunteers we have at our small facility always fall in love with our juvenile Corvids. We rear Crows and Magpies on a regular basis and these are such adorable babies that we have to keep a strict "no talking" policy in place with them so that they do not become tame. We also regularly rear Jackdaws but usually these are older and almost fledged.

When we were asked to take on a nest of Jackdaws, we were expecting the usual thin fledglings but what we saw on arrival was a nest of 4 very young hatchlings. Their nest had been illegally removed and dumped and the babies left to die.

Because they were cold and weak, the nestlings were immediately placed in an incubator set to a temperature of 35°. Once warm, they became more lively and eager to be fed. Rehydration fluids were mixed with the rearing mix to form a very runny paste in order to make it easier for

The hatchlings on arrival

them start digesting the food. The birds were given the runnier mix every half hour for the first few hours and it was gradually thickened up the normal consistency. Within a couple of days the Jackdaws were stronger and livelier.

Once the birds feathers started to come through we were able to reduce the temperature of their incubator to 30° and also begin to introduce finely chopped up chick to their diet so that they would grow good

feathers. They continued to grow well, without any problems and were soon standing and able to move around.

At this fledgling stage, they were given a small dish of chopped chick with a pinch of SA37 and also a bowl of cleaned white maggots. Jackdaws love insects and the maggots immediately gained the interest of the birds who began to pick them up and put them down without actually eating them.

After a few more days of handfeeding whilst tempting the birds with dog food, chopped chick and maggots, the birds were finally more interested in feeding themselves than being fed by us and so we decided to

introduce them to an aviary. For some reason, I always find that it is necessary to worm Blackbirds, Starlings and Corvids just before they go outside otherwise they begin to cough or sneeze, a symptom of them having a worm infestation. Pigeon wormers are fine for this at the recommended dose or Panacur 2.5% solution at a dose of 20mg/kg for 3 days. Once wormed, they were moved outside and had a great time fluttering around from perch to perch and digging through bark chips for dried mealworms.

The birds were kept in the aviary for 3 weeks until we were absolutely sure that they were competent flyers and then were allowed out via an open hatch in the aviary door one morning.

The birds, one by one, flew out of the aviary, but didn't go far at all before returning for food. The following morning, the same routine was followed and gradually the Jackdaws began to spend more time outside of the aviary and even roosted outside rather than coming back. This continued until eventually none of the birds were returning to the aviary. The birds continue to be fed locally but have now joined a much larger flock.

Our mischievous "Jacks" in their aviary

REARING WATERFOWL

Likely species that you will see

As there are so many different species in this family of birds, I have chosen the three most common species that you are likely to be asked to rear

MALLARD DUCK *(Anas platyrhynchos)*

GREYLAG GOOSE *(Anser anser)*

MUTE SWAN *(Cygnus olor)*

These birds are termed "precocial" meaning that they are independent at birth. Whilst they are able to feed themselves, they are not entirely independent as they need their mothers to keep them warm. Trying to reunite Mother and Baby is always a good idea if possible, particularly with Goslings and Cygnets who stay with their mothers far longer than ducklings.

A Gosling reunited with its parents

Also, young waterfowl are protected by oil from their mother's oil gland. They do not have the ability to generate this oil on their own. If they are placed in water they cannot get out of, they will eventually become waterlogged, chilled and die. Young ducks, geese and swans must NEVER be put in water.

We always keep smaller new arrivals in a loose fist to get their body temperature up and because we rear so many of these birds in a season, we use a puppy pen with a heat lamp hanging from the lid. If the birds are newly hatched, we will also provide them with a heat pad. If you are using a heatpad, this must be wrapped in a towel. I also find that a cuddly toy placed on top to hide under is much appreciated.

The cage should be lined with newspaper as waterfowl are very messy. You will need to clean them out 3 or 4 times per day. A poultry drinking bell is ideal for these birds so that they can drink the water but not get in it. If this is not available, a saucer with a tumbler glass placed top down in the middle will do the same job for very young ducklings though it will need filling up very regularly and will not be suitable for birds past 1 week old or for larger birds such as goslings or cygnets.

Cygnets

Waterfowl should never be allowed to run out of drinking water and their food, a proprietary chick crumb available from farm shops, should be placed in a shallow dish near to the water so that they can dabble. As soon as they are large enough to take it, add cracked corn to their diet and some greens, such as finely shredded cabbage.

When they have a good supply of feathers, at around 5 weeks of age for ducklings and longer for cygnets and goslings, you can start introducing them to water to paddle in. We tend to take our ducklings out into the garden during the day where I have a large pen with various shallow water baths for them to play in.

I start them off with a fairly small tray of water and gradually move up to bigger ones as they grow in confidence. This gives them time to experience the sounds and temperatures outside whilst keeping them safe. They should not be left unsupervised or left unsecured at night and should preferably be brought back inside at night if not completely feathered.

Ducklings cannot be released until they are at least 8 weeks old. Cygnets and Goslings stay with their parents until they are around 3 months old. If you have a lone duckling, cygnet or gosling, find a rehabber with another one so that they can be reared together. Any lake or river where no fishing or shooting is allowed will be suitable for release.

Angel Wing

This is a condition that causes the wing joint to twist out at an angle causing the feathers to stand out away from the body. It is not a terminal injury but it will mean that the bird is unable to fly.

There is some conjecture about whether the cause is genetic or dietary. Research by the Wildlife Trust has shown that feeding waterfowl on an unlimited, high protein, diet causes them to grow at a faster rate than is natural. This, in turn puts added weight and pressure on the joints which simply cannot cope with it. My own personal belief is that even if a whole clutch of ducklings is fed only on an inappropriate high protein diet, only one or two of the ducklings will get the condition. Therefore, those birds that are genetically prone to the condition will develop it if fed on the wrong diet.

We take no chances and add corn and greens to our waterfowl diet as soon as the birds are able to take it and we never feed our birds on bread. If caught early enough it is possible to support the affected wing with splints and strapping. Once the bird's diet is changed, the wing should straighten and grow normally.

WATERFOWL – Case Study

Each Year, we rear dozens of Mallard Ducklings, so when someone called regarding three small ducklings that they had found wandering around a yard, we simply assumed that they would be yet more Mallards to add to our existing broods.

When the ducklings arrived, we were surprised to see small black and white balls of fluff appear from under jumper where they had been kept warm on their journey.

We have to confess that none of us knew what species the ducklings were, but as with any other duckling, we knew that they needed warmth, food and water and so they were made comfortable in a pen with a brooder lamp, a bowl of chick crumbs and a water bell.

One of the young Shelducks on arrival

A few days later, one of our volunteers arrived to clean out and informed us that they were in fact young Shelducks. The Shelduck is a large sized duck. It is an extremely attractive species which is common around the coastline of Britain. It is a migratory bird and the adults arrive at their breeding areas during the late winter or early spring. After breeding the parents of the young will leave them in "crèches" supervised by just a small group of adults and return to their moulting grounds.

Aged 2 weeks

Since we are located in a distinctly inland area, we can only assume that these ducklings were being cared for in a "crèche" when they became separated from the group and were lost.

All 3 ducklings progressed well and were soon big enough for us to add cracked corn and some greens to their diet.

At the age of 5 weeks, the birds were developing a good supply of feathers and were taken outside for their first introduction to swimming. We have a 10' by 8' pen in the garden that we keep specifically for ducklings. It has a hutch type house filled with straw at one end and a large plastic tub sunk into the ground at the other end for swimming. Of course, they took to swimming like to proverbial "ducks to water".

On the first morning we stayed with the ducklings whilst they were in the water just to make sure that they did not chill. They all jumped straight into the water and began to wash and preen. Clearly, it was exhausting work as they all got out after a short while and huddled together in the sun to dry off.

The Ducklings were brought back in to their indoor pen that night and after a few more days of being taken outside and then brought back in at night, we decided to just herd them into the straw filled house at night and lock them in securely with food and water.

The ducks continued to be let out of the house in the mornings and put away at night until they were 8 weeks old and ready for release. In the meantime, we had been speaking to the local Wildlife Trust who informed us that their Reserve at nearby Tring was on the migratory path of Shelducks and would be perfect for them.

Early on a Sunday morning, we met the Wildlife Trust staff at the reserve and released the ducks into a shallow area. We stayed with them for a couple of hours, just watching them enjoying the water and as they swam off into deeper water, we left them to it.

The following week, we were informed by the staff that all 3 were doing well and had been joined by others.

The group on release

REARING GAMEBIRDS

Likely species that you will see

GREY PARTRIDGE *(Perdix perdix)*
PHEASANT *(Phasianus colchicus)*
RED LEGGED PARTRIDGE *(Alectoris rufa)*
QUAIL *(Coturnix coturnix)*

Gamebirds are semi-precocial in the wild, ie they are fully mobile but are shown food to peck at and are brooded. When we have had lone chicks brought in to us they will most times not eat any food offered and will starve to death if intervening action is not taken.

We have found that the best method of feeding these birds is with a mini pastette and Tropican Breeding Mash or Kaytee Exact Handrearing Formula. Hold the bird loosely in a fist and put the tip of the pipette to the tip of

Juvenile pheasant

the beak. Squeeze a little of the formula onto the end of the beak until the bird gets the hang of it. If this does not work, get someone else to hold the bird whilst you, very gently, open the beak and squeeze a tiny drop into the mouth. Repeat this until the bird does get the idea. You will want to get about 1 ml of the formula into the bird every hour from 7am to 8pm to begin with. You MUST be careful to do this very slowly. If the bird inhales the formula rather than swallowing it, it is likely to die. A similar bedding set up to that used for ducklings will be ideal. A towel covered heatpad for the bird is very important and as they tend to be very shy, a cuddly toy that they can hide under is good too.

Juvenile partridge

You will have to increase the amount of food as the bird grows and you are aiming to give it 10% of its bodyweight at each feed. Try sprinkling some chick crumbs and insect food (Bogena) around the cage between feeds so that as they grow, the chicks will instinctively peck at them and realise that they are food. A shallow dish of water should always be available too.

As they grow bigger and become fully feathered they will begin to peck at food. Seeds and layers mash are ideal for them as well as grit, insect mix and mealworms. All Pheasants and Partridges just adore dried mealworms! All are available from a good poultry supplier. As with all other birds, these will need time in an aviary to adjust to the sights, sounds and temperatures of the outside world. When the birds are grown enough for release at around 8 weeks, you must be sure to find them a place where there are other birds of the same species. A lone bird will not survive for long. Also, make sure that they are released well away from shooting sites or your good work will all go to waste.

GAMEBIRDS: - Case Study

We now quite frequently get Pheasant chicks in during the Summer and when we received a call from a lady who thought she'd found a baby chicken, we were pretty sure that it would be a pheasant chick that arrived.

Like ducklings, any stragglers from the brood are simply left behind and for some reason the chick had become separated from the rest of its family. They are generally exhausted by the time they're brought in and this chick was no exception.

She was placed in a zoozone cage with overhead lamp and a thermometer inside told us that they temperature was the required 30°. There were nice fluffy towels and a cuddly toy for the bird to hide under and the bird was warmed up and then given fluids at the rate of 0.5mls per hour which gradually had Tropican breeding mash added to it.

Lone chicks are often distressed and as soon as she was strong enough, the lonely cheeping began. Luckily for us, somebody called in later that day to say that they had also found a chick. This one was slightly older and was the perfect company for our chick.

Company at last!

What was really great was that the older chick was already able to feed herself and so our chick immediately began to copy. From that point on, the chicks happily pecked at chick crumbs, insect mix and dried mealworms, whilst the youngest continued to have supplemental feeds every 3 hours just to make sure she was getting everything she needed.

The birds grew beautifully from that point onward and were soon replacing soft down with beautifully marked feathers. We then received a phone call from another wildlife rescue organisation who also had a lone Pheasant chick and so that one came to join our 2.

In the meantime, we had been invited to release the birds into some private gardens where they would be able to live safely and also be fed daily. This was an amazing opportunity and at the age of 2 months, the 3 birds went to live in the gardens where they remain today.

Release day!

REARING BIRDS OF PREY

SPECIES	FAMILY	NATURAL FOOD
BARN OWL (Tyto alba)	OWLS	Voles and Mice
BUZZARD (Buteo buteo)	HAWKS	Small Mammals, Birds and Carrion
GOSHAWK (Accipiter gentilis)	HAWKS	Birds and Mammals
HOBBY (Falco subbuteo)	FALCONS	Insects and Small Birds
KESTREL (Falco tinnunculus)	FALCONS	Small Mammals
LITTLE OWL (Athene noctuna)	OWLS	Small Mammals, Birds and Insects
LONG EARED OWL (Asio otus)	OWLS	Small Mammals and Birds
MERLIN (Falco columbarius)	FALCONS	Small Birds
PEREGRINE (Falco peregrinus)	FALCONS	Medium sized birds
RED KITE (Milvus milvus)	HAWK	Small Mammals and Carrion
SPARROWHAWK (Accipiter nisus)	HAWK	Small Birds
TAWNY OWL (Strix Aluco)	OWLS	Small Mammals, Birds, Frogs & Lizards

Many of the birds mentioned above will only be seen in rescue centres in certain parts of the Country and some are species of conservation concern and will need to go into a very carefully monitored release programme via the RSPB or similar organisation. For example, **The releasing of captive bred Barn Owls into the wild is an illegal offence. You will need to find an organisation that holds a licence for the release of Barn Owls in order to make sure that your bird has the best chance of survival.**

Juvenile Barn Owl

Birds of Prey include Falcons, Hawks and Owls. They are at the top of the food chain in the bird world and have exceptional eyesight for hunting. It is vital that all Birds of Prey receive fur, feather and bone in their diet. Failure to offer them this diet, will lead to severe problems in their bone development that will be irreversible.

Only the very youngest of Birds of Prey will require an additional heat source (under 2 weeks of age). I use a pet carrier with a cat comforter heat pad at the bottom. The heat pad is covered with a layer of newspaper and a towel and another towel is then twisted into a ring to form the makeshift nest. It is very important that Birds of Prey have their feet tucked under them inside the nest ring to avoid splayed legs.

As with Corvids, it is not really possible to offer these birds their natural diet and is not actually a good idea as you may be passing on unnecessary parasites or even poisons by doing so. We use the only alternative available which is day old hatchery chicks which must be chopped up, using a pair of kitchen scissors. You will need to remove the head, legs and egg sac for most juvenile Birds of Prey and for those very young birds, less than about 10 days old, you will need to feed them only the muscle, and organs of the chick, introducing down and then very slowly over the following couple of weeks.

Offering the piece of chick, dipped in rehydration fluid with a pair of plastic forceps is usually enough to get the bird to grab at the food and eat it. If not, you will need to gently open the mouth and put the food to the back of the throat. You should also sprinkle a pinch of SA37 vitamin powder on to the chopped pieces before offering it to the bird as this will help them grow strong bones and feathers. Do not give fluids directly to the bird; dipping the chick in fluids will be enough.

The bird should be fed the parts of 1 chick (2 for the larger birds such as Buzzards) every 3-4 hours from 7am to 7pm (Smaller birds, such as kestrels can be fed at the same intervals but on smaller amounts). The Bird should regurgitate pellets frequently. Weigh your baby bird every day and increase the amount of food as the bird grows. You are aiming to see a 10% increase in bodyweight each day. This should be the only time you handle the bird and should be done as quickly as possible.

When weaning Birds of Prey you will need to find them food as close to their natural diet as possible. Dark coloured defrosted mice should be offered to Barn Owls, Little Owls, Tawny Owls and Kestrels in small chopped pieces at first. Defrosted Rats can be offered to larger Birds of Prey such as Buzzards and Kites. Sparrowhawks, Merlin's and Hobby's can continue to be offered chicks, as other small birds are not available, but the chicks should be opened up (cut open along the chest cavity) so that the bird of prey is able to recognise other prey in due course. By the time your bird has grown a good supply of adult feathers and is picking up food by itself (timing will vary according to species but some are as early as 2 weeks old), it is time to move the bird into an aviary and prepare it for release.

The ever grumpy Little Owl!

There is some contention over whether Birds of Prey are taught to hunt by their parents or whether the hunting instinct is natural. However, you want to give your bird the absolute best chance at a successful life in the wild and so it is best to use a very soft release technique with birds of prey. This soft release process can take a few weeks and you will have no contact with the bird whatsoever during the process.

It is usual for some birds of prey not to move too far from their nest site, so you must be sure that the release process is carried out in a suitable area. Make sure you are aware of your birds needs. You will need to know it's hunting techniques and be sure that there is a supply of natural prey at the site before going ahead. You will need to work with other organisations or a falconer, if your own location is unsuitable for the bird. For example, Tawny owls, Hobby's and sparrowhawks need woodland, Little owls, Buzzards, Kites and Kestrels need open spaces such as parkland or farmland.

It is absolutely essential when rearing wild birds of prey that you have an aviary or hacking shed. The aviary will need to have one solid side so that the bird cannot see you approach as it MUST NOT associate you with the supply of food. If you have an aviary, you can improvise just with a piece of ply board. The aviary will also need a hatch that can be opened for the bird to leave in due course, preferably a sky hatch, which can also be used for the provision of food. The size of the aviary will depend upon the size of your bird, but you will need space for the bird to practice flying and building up flight muscles. Food should be made available at the hatch for the bird during its natural hunting hours. Approach from the blocked side so that the bird does not see you. Give the bird time to get used to feeding at the hatch and observing it's surroundings, 4 to 5 weeks should be sufficient. When you are sure that the bird is ready, you can leave the hatch open after feeding at the appropriate time, so that the bird can leave and return as it wishes. Continue to provide food for the bird until it is no longer taken.

THESE ARE PROBABLY THE MOST DIFFICULT FAMILY OF BIRDS TO HAND REAR AND RELEASE AS THEY EACH HAVE SPECIAL REQUIREMENTS. DO NOT BE AFRAID TO ASK FOR HELP. AS LONG AS THE BIRD IS NOT TAME, MOST OTHER ORGANISATIONS WILL BE PLEASED TO ASSIST YOU.

Juvenile Hobby – we sought help from the RSPB to give this bird the best chance it could have.

BIRDS OF PREY – Case Study

During one Summer season, three Tawny Owl chicks were brought in to us in quick succession. Each of the chicks was around the same age of 5-6 weeks old.

One of the chicks was found in the road and brought in presumed to have been hit by a car, one was found lying next to another owl, who had died and the other, found at the base of a tree really shouldn't have been picked up at all as it was no doubt "branching". Unfortunately, with no details of where the owl was found (it was taken into a vet's office and left there), we were unable to return the bird and left with no option but to rear all three.

The first two chicks were each cold and weak and were warmed up on a heat pad nest, before being fed "little and often" feeds of chopped chick dipped in rehydration fluid, to combat malnutrition and dehydration. The third chick had good feather covering, was warm and not dehydrated and therefore did not need a further source of heat, though for ease and convenience, he was fed on the same time schedule as the other two chicks. Being weaker, the first two birds, were easier to feed and readily accepted the chicks, the third was not so happy and required restraint in a towel and the food wiped along his beak to stimulate him to grab. After a couple of days, all three chicks had realised that the food being offered was a good thing and took the food from a pair of plastic tweezers.

Over the following three weeks the birds were weighed daily and shown to be gaining their required amount of weight each day. All 3 were taking food readily and growing feathers that were in good condition. All three were also clicking at anyone who approached them and would not tolerate being handled at all.

At about 8-10 weeks of age, the three owls were transferred into an aviary in a quiet corner of the garden. Our garden is situated at the edge of a housing estate, with a woodland path leading in one direction to a huge park and in the other direction to open fields. There is an abundance of mice and voles in the area (a

Another 2 chicks arrive

study shown of local cat predatory patterns has proven this), so the territory was perfect for the owls and no other Tawny owls at that time were known to be in the area.

All three were taken into the aviary late afternoon on a warm mid-July day and immediately went to the very top corner of the aviary and huddled together. As it was an extremely warm night, it was felt safe to leave them out overnight though they were checked on at midnight to make sure that all three were still off the ground and looking comfortable. Food, a mix of chopped and whole chick and mouse, for the first night, was left for them on an upended log in the middle of the aviary to make it as easy as possible for the owls to find it and sure enough, in the morning the food was gone and the owls were back up in their corner, huddled together with their backs to us.

The same procedure was followed for the next few days until the birds were comfortable and then the chopped food was stopped and only whole chicks and mice were left out for them. This too was gone the following day so food began to be left around the aviary in various places to make sure that the birds were capable of seeking it out and when this was working well and the birds were felt ready for preparation for their release.

Although only 1 person had had any access to the aviary, a screen was erected around the side of the aviary and only the door and the hatch above it were left uncovered. As this was protected by the nesting box of the aviary and meant that the birds could not see, this was deemed the acceptable route for food delivery. A food ledge had also been made, prior to the birds taking up residence, at the hatch in the lower half of the apex roof over the door and the food was from now on left at the hatch only. Each morning the food was checked to make sure it was gone and each evening at dusk, more food was left out. This process went on for another 4 weeks until the beginning of September, which is when Tawny Owls in the wild would begin to become independent.

A night was decided upon for release and a night vision camera set up. The hatch was left open after the night time feed and the birds were left to it. All three of the birds left the aviary in quick succession and were seen (with the aid of the night vision equipment) sitting in the trees around the aviary for a while before one flew off and was quickly followed by the others.

Though none of the birds returned to the aviary following release, food was put out again for the birds the following evening and one of the birds was seen to return and take it.

Thereafter, none of the birds returned for any of the food left out but three owls were seen flying over the roof of the house, some few days later. Though we did not radio tag the owls, none had ever been heard in the vicinity of the area previous to the

Our 3 chicks, almost ready to go

release of our three owls and screeches and the familiar twit-twoo of Tawny Owls is now a most familiar sound from dusk onwards, usually within just a few feet of the release aviary.

BIRDS OF PREY – Case Study 2

We were contacted by a local Golf Course early one morning in June and asked if we could help 3 Kestrel chicks that had been thrown from their nest box.

The course had been vandalised by joyriders the previous evening and it would seem that a purpose built nest box had been targeted by the vandals. Other than being slightly cold, the chicks were unharmed and our first thought was to try and reunite them with their parents. We took the chicks in and warmed them up while the golf course owners attempted to re-erect the nest box. Later on that day we were advised that the parents had been seen by the course owners but that sadly, the joyriders had also been back. At that time, we decided that it was just too risky to put the chicks back in that situation.

The parents had done a wonderful job of caring for the 3 chicks, all of whom were fat and healthy. They were not at all happy about our presence which was great as we needed them to stay as wild as possible. Within a very short time of arriving the chicks were feeding themselves from a bowl of chopped chick and we were able to stay as far away from them as we could. Their weight was monitored daily

Growing some nice feathers

As soon as their plumage had grown through, the chicks were moved into a large aviary at the very end of one of our volunteer's gardens. The front of the aviary was blocked off so that they couldn't see her at all and they were fed via a hatch in the door.

Into pre-release

After 3 weeks in the aviary, the hatch was opened and........nothing! All 3 chicks stayed firmly put until the following day when one by one they ventured out and disappeared. None of the chicks returned to the aviary despite food being left out for them. However, juvenile Kestrels do stay together for quite some time and our volunteer, Jenny continued to see the 3 still together for at least a month after release.

REARING WADERS

Likely species that you will see

COOT *(Fulica atra)*

WATER RAIL *(Rallus aquaticus)*

LAPWING *(Vanellus vanellus)*

WOODCOCK *(Scolopax rusticola)*

MOORHEN *(Gallinula chloropus)*

PLOVER (Charadrius dubius)

SNIPE *(Gallinago gallinago)*

Our young Moorhen Chick on arrival

Like pheasants, Moorhens and Coots are semi-precocial and will feed if shown how to by their mothers. However, also like Pheasants, when they are brought into captivity, they will often starve if just left to it.

We use the same method with coots and moorhens as with pheasant chicks. However, instead of Tropican/Kaytee we use our rearing mix to feed these species of birds.

Using exactly the same method as for pheasants, hold the bird loosely in a fist and put the tip of the pipette to the tip of the beak. Squeeze a little of the formula onto the end of the beak until the bird gets the hang of it. If this does not work, get someone else to hold the bird whilst you, very gently, open the beak and squeeze a tiny drop into the mouth. Repeat this until the bird does get the idea. You will want to get about 1 ml of the formula into the bird every hour from 7am to 8pm to begin with. You MUST be careful to do this very slowly. If the bird inhales the formula rather than swallowing it, it is likely to die.

These birds will also definitely need a source of heat, ie a covered heatpad or brooder lamp and we tend to keep them in incubator type cages when very small (at around 30°to start with and a tented towel that they can hide under as they are very shy birds. A deep sided dish of cleaned (48 hour fridge starved) maggots is necessary for these birds. They will be drawn by the movement of the maggots and encouraged to peck at them. Until you are sure that they are pecking at the maggots and eating them however, continue to pastette feed 1 ml every hour as before.

As the bird grows, continue to feed on clean maggots and mix in chick crumbs and either Bogena Universal Insect Mix or Haiths Prosecto. Remember these are water birds (with the exception of the Woodcock) so a continuous supply of fresh water is necessary. Start off with a shallow saucer with a tumbler glass placed top down in the middle so that the bird cannot get in it, though it will need filling up very regularly and will only be suitable for the first week before a larger bell drinker will be necessary. Once the bird is bigger a large tray of water can be provided in addition to the drinker for "paddling" and greens such as watercress and dried mealworms can be added to encourage the bird to feed.

Once the bird is fully feathered it can be moved to an outside aviary to acclimatise to the weather. There should be water in the enclosure. We use a large 1 meter square, 15cm deep tray, sunk into a base of bark chips so that the bird can get used to foraging and wading. Alternatively, a child's plastic sandpit would also work. Use only shallow water (these are waders not swimmers) and to start with, provide a ramp or "step" so that the bird can get in and out easily.

You will also need to provide areas for the moorhen to hide. A small hutch covered with foliage works quite well for us. The bird will need to stay in the enclosure for 2 weeks before being released at a suitable riverside location where no fishing takes place.

The same Moorhen 3 weeks later.

WADERS – Case Study

On arrival, the tiny Lapwing chick

We were contacted by a member of the local Bird Club during May about a young Lapwing chick that he had found in an unusual location. The finder had been leaving the Motorway service station when he saw the chick running around on the slip road. Knowing he couldn't leave the bird there, he stopped and picked up the bird and then contacted us.

The bird, who was very nervous, was given a heatpad and a quiet enclosed cage so that she could calm down and warm up.

Once warm she was gavaged with rehydration fluid and given a bowl of Maggots and Insect food. Unfortunately, she didn't show any interest in the food and so we had to disturb her again in order to feed her. We then left her alone with her food in a quiet part of the hospital. When we checked on her an hour later, the food had all been eaten.

Starting to get some feather growth.

From that point on, only one person cleaned the cage at the end of the day when everything was quiet and aside from that the bird was left alone in her pen with a water tray and her food. This seemed to be absolutely fine with her and within just a month she was ready to move outside.

She was put in our quietest aviary and had her small shallow pool, a hutch to hide in and lots of grubs scattered amongst the bark chips. As it was so warm, after just one week, we felt she would be better out of out environment and off to release.

We contacted The Wildlife Trust who made an exception to their usual rule and allowed us to release her at one of the Reserves which had a huge flock of Lapwings.

So at 8 am on a sunny July morning the Lapwing was released onto the Reserve and after a little paddle flew straight into the middle of her new flock.

REARING SPECIALIST FEEDERS - SWIFTS

Swifts migrate to Britain in May and make their return flight to Africa during August and you might think that you should find this bird in the section about Insect eating garden birds, especially as House Martins and swallows are found there. However, unlike their relatives, swifts are completely unable to be weaned as they eat and sleep on the wing and are unable to pick up food from the floor or a dish.

When you find an adult bird that has been grounded, it will not be able to take flight again due to the shortness of its legs and the length of its wings. The bird may simply need some food and rehydration before being released again, but should be checked over by someone qualified. Keep it in a high sided box and line the sides with a towel or kitchen roll so that the swift can grip on it vertically. After a few feeds, if the swift weighs around 40g and is moving around a lot, you can release it (see below)

A small amount of Bogena Universal Insect Food or Haiths Prosecto and SA37 vitamin powder mixed with mashed maggots (the maggots must be starved in the fridge for 1 or 2 days until the black line in the centre of them has disappeared) are a good source of food. An equally good source of additional food is zoo meds small can 'o' crickets or can'o'pillars which can be used to supplement the maggot diet.

To feed both adults and juvenile swifts, roll the maggot mix into a small ball between your fingers (about 8mm in diameter). Wrap the swift in a small towel so that none of the food is spilled on the feathers (this will also stop the bird flapping about, if it is an adult). Gently open the delicate beak by sliding a nail in and then holding the mouth open, dip the maggot ball into some water, shake it off and then pop it to the back of the throat. If you do not put it right to the back of the throat, the swift will spit it out again! Repeat this 5 times and feed the swift every 2 hours from 7am to 8pm (a smaller quantity if very young). Eventually, the swift (if juvenile) will open its mouth to you, making the job much simpler.

A young swiftlet

When very young Swifts will need a heated area (between 30° and 35° depending on age) and will be happy in a nest bowl. As the swift grows provide it with a towel lined plastic box so that it can climb up and hang on to the sides.

You cannot release juvenile swifts until they weigh 45g and have their full flight feathers which are about 16cm long.

The swift will not wean and should be hand fed right up to the point of release. To release a swift, take it to an open space and hold it high up in the air on the flat of your palm. The bird should fly away and instinct will soon take over.

Almost ready to go!

REARING SPECIALIST FEEDERS - WOODPECKERS

There are only 3 species of Woodpecker in the UK and in size order from largest to smallest, they are: Green Woodpecker, Great Spotted Woodpecker and the rare Lesser Spotted Woodpecker.

All 3 are Woodland specialists and tend only to visit gardens in the harsher Winter months. The reason that I have included them under Specialist Feeders is because they feed almost exclusively on Insects and have those great feet adapted for tree climbing, plus awesome beaks and long tongues used for drilling holes and seeking out insects.

I have successfully reared Great Spotted Woodpeckers from nestling age and, just recently,

Fledgling Great Spotted Woodpecker

Green Woodpeckers from hatchling age and so will share what I noticed during those experiences. Obviously with nestlings, a lot of the hard work has been done by the parents and overcoming the stress of their captivity is the main goal in getting them to eat. I have always found that a dish of "cleaned" maggots in a deep sided dish will work eventually, with Great Spotted Woodpeckers but that they do respond well to the rearing mix fed out of a suet holder/log, so that they can probe.

Our Green Woodpeckers were Hatchlings when brought in, just a few days old (they had been inside a dead tree that was cut down) and they were therefore placed straight in an incubator set to 35°

Once rehydrated and alert, the first interesting thing I noted about them is that they didn't "gape" as such. It was pretty easy to get them to respond to feeds of rearing mix via a 1ml Pastette however. A gentle tap on the beak with

Hatchling Green Woodpeckers

the pastette soon had them grabbing for it or probing with their lizard-like tongues. When feeding it is important to have the pastette past the glottis (the opening to the trachea at the back of the tongue) but not to push the pastette down the throat.

All 4 of our Green Wood pecker chicks grew well on their new diet and were growing beautiful feathers. Hand feeds were every 30 minutes (about 1ml of food per feed) to start off with from 7am to 10pm and eventually reduced back to every hour and up to 3 mls of food per feed.

Once the birds began to leave the nest we gave them logs to climb up on but noticed that they were not interested at all in any food placed in the cage and so they continued to be hand fed, although food such as insect rearing mix, cleaned maggots and prosecto was also available to them at all times. This hand feeding continued even whilst in the aviary until eventually we actually saw the Woodpeckers feeding themselves on the insect mix from the suet log.

At this point, we were finally able to begin to withdraw from them and 2 weeks later their hatch was opened and one by one they left the aviary. The hatch was left open for them and their food was hung on the outside of the aviary.

Two of the chicks stayed around the garden for far longer than the others and even continued to return to the aviary for another couple of weeks for food. Thankfully, they have a very distinctive call and we were able to hear them quite frequently. Interestingly, they never did bother with the maggots or the insect mix, preferring only their rearing mix from the log, though having watched them in the trees I've seen first hand that they are able to forage perfectly well for insects there.

Finally showing interest in feeding themselves

REARING SPECIALIST FEEDERS - GULLS

We had our first Gull chicks brought in to us in 2008 and they have become the firm favourites of our volunteers ever since. Our first batch were from a colony of lesser black backed gulls and herring gulls who have taken to nesting upon the flat rooftop of a local factory and inevitably some of the tiny chicks had fallen off.

The Gull chicks on arrival

We had 3 chicks brought in to us in just one week. As each had fallen off of the edge of the building it was impossible to determine which of the dozens of nests they had come from and we were not therefore able to put the chicks back with their parents.

Aside from being shocked, each of the chicks was miraculously unharmed and once in an incubator set at 30° each was keen to grab at chopped pieces of chick from forceps.

We decided that our baby bird rearing mix would suffice for the rearing of these youngsters with one or two modifications. The mix was made up as usual though in a slightly thicker form and also had pieces of chopped chick mixed in. Gull chicks are semi precocial and though they were fed from forceps to begin with to get them used to the food, after a couple of days they were left with a bowl of the mix which they attacked with great gusto.

Each chick was weighed daily and we aimed to feed each one around 10-15% of their bodyweight each day. All three birds grew with no difficultly at all and were soon able to be put out into the garden during the day with a small area of water in which to preen their forming feathers and move around to strengthen their muscles.

At about 4 weeks of age, they were given fish in addition to their insect/chick mix and were also moved to a larger pen with a deeper pool, in order to make sure the coming feathers were preened and oiled properly.

As their down disappeared and their feathers grew through, we had to begin to consider where we would release the birds. Gull chicks are independent fairly early on and do not rely on their parents once able to fly and feed themselves completely.

Our choices were to put them back with the colony they had come from or to take them down to the coast.

By releasing them back at the site that they were found we had to consider that they would be likely to stay there permanently and may become considered as a nuisance, particularly as they had already been reared by humans and would therefore associate humans with food even though they were in no way tame.

We decided that a coastal release would be better for the birds which were by now eating well, were a great weight, fully waterproofed and fully feathered. However, our hand reared birds could not just be left at the seaside, so we had to look into getting the assistance of a rehabilitator on the coast that would be able to help include them in a soft release.

After some ringing around, we found a larger organisation used to rearing hundreds of gulls who were more than happy to take on our 3 fledglings and join them with a group getting ready for release on the South coast and so we made the journey over to the centre with our chicks and bid them farewell. We received a later update that all of the chicks were soft released into a large colony.

As a small "rehabber" you will almost certainly need to work with other organisations at some time. We have always found most of the other larger organisations to be extremely friendly and accommodating as long as you are doing the job right and the bird is fit, healthy and above all wild.

Just a couple of weeks later, what a difference!

APPENDIX 1 – Legislation Schedule 4

BIRDS WHICH MUST BE REGISTERED AND RINGED IF KEPT IN CAPTIVITY

Common name	Scientific name
Bunting, Cirl	Emberiza cirlus
Bunting, Lapland	Calcarius lapponicus
Bunting, Snow	Plectrophenax nivalis
Chough	Pyrrhocorax pyrrhocorax
Crossbills (all species)	Loxia
Falcons (all species)]	Falconidae
Fieldfare	Turdus pilaris
Firecrest	Regulus ignicapillus
Hawks, True (except Old world vultures) that is to say, Buzzards, Eagles, Harriers, Hawks and Kites (all species in each case)]	Accipitridae (except the genera Aegypius, Gypaetus, Gypohierax, Gyps, Neophron, Sarcogyps and Trigonoceps)
Oriole, Golden	Oriolus oriolus
Osprey	Pandion haliaetus
Redstart, Black	Phoenicurus ochruros
Redwing	Turdus iliacus
Serin	Serinus serinus
Shorelark	Eremophila alpestris
Shrike, Red-backed	Lanius collurio
Tit, Bearded	Panurus biarmicus
Tit, Crested	Parus cristatus
Warbler, Cetti's	Cettia cetti
Warbler, Dartford	Sylvia undata
Warbler, Marsh	Acrocephalus palustris
Warbler, Savi's	Locustella Liscinioides
Woodlark	Lullula arborea
Wryneck	Jynx torquilla
Any bird one of whose parents or other lineal ancestor was a bird of a kind specified in the foregoing provisions of this Schedule.]	

APPENDIX 1 – LEGISLATION Schedule 9

BIRDS THAT IT IS ILLEGAL TO RELEASE INTO THE WILD IN THE UK

Common name	Scientific name
Budgerigar	Melopsittacus undulatus
Capercaillie	Tetrao urogallus
Duck, Carolina Wood	Aix sponsa
Duck, Mandarin	Aix galericulata
Duck, Ruddy	Oxyura jamaicensis
Eagle, White-tailed	Haliaetus albicilla
Goose, Canada	Branta canadensis
Goose, Egyptian	Alopochen aegyptiacus
Heron, Night	Nycticorax nycticorax
Parakeet, Ring-necked	Psittacula krameri
Partridge, Chukar	Alectoris chukar
Partridge, Rock	Alectoris graeca
Pheasant, Golden	Chrysolophus pictus
Pheasant, Lady Amherst's	Chrysolophus amherstiae
Pheasant, Reeves'	Syrmaticus reevesii
Pheasant, Silver	Lophura nycthemera
Quail, Bobwhite	Colinus virginianus
Owl, Barn	Tyto alba

APPENDIX 2 - EMERGENCY FEEDING GUIDES

These emergency feeding guides are exactly that. They will suffice for one or two feeds only until the recommended diet can be obtained.

BIRDS OF PREY

Day old frozen chicks are widely available from farm shops, good pet stores, and reptile stores. If you cannot find any, obtain a can of feline a/d and a 20 ml syringe from your vet. Mix the a/d with a little water and VERY slowly syringe the mix into the bird's mouth. These birds need chopped chicks or chopped mice asap.

GARDEN BIRDS – INSECT EATERS

Mash up a can of chicken flavoured pedigree chum, mixed in a blender with water to form a smooth paste and use the flat end of a teaspoon handle or a blunted cocktail stick to feed the bird. Do not dig for worms as the gut contents of these can sometimes be toxic to baby birds.

GARDEN BIRDS – SEED EATERS

As above - Mash up a can of chicken flavoured pedigree chum, mixed in a blender with water to form a smooth paste and use the flat end of a teaspoon handle or a blunted cocktail stick to feed the bird. Do not dig for worms as the gut contents of these can sometimes be toxic to baby birds.

GARDEN BIRDS – CROP FEEDERS

Ready Brek or soaked porridge oats, blended to a fine paste will work as a temporary measure but does not have the required vitamins to be used on a long term basis. If you do not have the equipment to crop feed, brown bread, soaked in water and rolled between finger and thumb can be inserted into the mouth towards the back of the throat – for older chicks only. Alternatively defrosted peas can be used in the same way. You will need to do this approximately 10 - 20 times per feed. It is stressful for the bird and should be used for only one or two feeds.

CORVIDS

A mashed up quality dog food is fine, but should be mixed with a vitamin powder such as SA37 and fur/feather must be introduced as soon as possible.

WATERFOWL

Brown bread soaked in water will suffice on a very short term basis

GAMEBIRDS

Ready brek or soaked porridge oats, blended to a fine paste and fed to the chick from a blunted cocktail stick will suffice as a temporary measure. You will need to feed the bird about 1ml every couple of hours and so this method will be time consuming.

APPENDIX 3 - WHERE TO BUY EQUIPMENT AND FEED

Most these items can be easily found on the internet and many of them can be purchased from ebay.

Plastic Tanks – Any good quality pet store, zoozone cages are preferred

Heat Pad – Challoner Cat Comforter - www.challoner-marketing.com

Brooder Lamp – Reptiles Stores - www.theincubatorshop.co.uk

Brinsea Incubator - www.theincubatorshop.co.uk

Plastic Dishes – Any good supermarket

Virkon Disinfectant - www.sphsupplies.co.uk

Frozen chicks – Any good pet store, farm shop or www.honeybrookfarm.com

Bogena Universal Bird Food – Good pet stores or www.ukpetsupplies.com

Haiths Prosecto – www.haiths.com

Avipro – Good pet stores or www.sphsupplies.co.uk

SA37 – Good pet stores, such as Pets at Home

Vetzyme Stress – Available from your vet or www.petmeds.co.uk

Kaytee Exact Handfeeding Formula for parrots - www.24parrot.com

Tropican Breeding Mash - www.24parrot.com

Catac Teats – http://www.catac.co.uk or www.sphsupplies.co.uk

Syringes – Available from your vet or www.sphsupplies.co.uk

Stainless Steel Crop Tubes – www.birdcareco.com

Flexible Crop Tubes – www.vetark.co.uk

Plastic Forceps/ Tweezers – www.ebay.co.uk or www.firstaid4sport.co.uk

Drinkers and Chick crumbs – Any good pet store or farm shop or ebay.

Pipettes and Pastettes – http://www.alphalabs.co.uk

Can O Crickets - http://www.livefoodsdirect.co.uk

Maggots – any good fishing store

Applaws Dried Kitten food 80% chicken – www.applaws.co.uk

Ready made rearing mix – contact info@wildlife-rescue.org.uk

APPENDIX 4 – ZOONOSES

Whilst you are extremely unlikely to catch anything at all from your bird, it would be irresponsible not to mention the possibility however remote it may be.

The following are a list of Zoonoses to be aware of:-

Psittacosis (Ornithosis, Chlamydiosis): Psittacosis is caused by the bacteria *Chlamydia psittaci*. C. Infected birds are highly contagious to other birds and can also pass on infection to humans. The organism is spread to humans by direct contact with secretions from infected animals. Typical symptoms in the bird are diarrhoea, ocular discharge, and nasal discharge.

The infection in humans by *C.psittaci*, can cause fever, headache, myalgia chills, and upper and lower respiratory disease. Serious complications can occur and include pneumonia, hepatitis, myocarditis, thrombophlebitis and encephalitis. It is responsive to antibiotic therapy but relapses can occur in untreated infections.

Newcastle Disease: Newcastle disease is caused by a paramyxovirus and can be seen in birds both wild and domestic. Transmission is mainly airborne but contaminated food, water and equipment can also transmit the infection within bird colonies. Pathogenic strains produce anorexia and respiratory disease in adult birds. Young birds often show neurological signs. In humans the disease is characterized by conjunctivitis, fever, and respiratory symptoms.

Good personal-hygiene practices which include hand washing after handling animals or their waste should be in place.

Salmonella: Along with a variety of other species, *Salmonella,* and other enteric bacteria are capable of causing disease in humans. Salmonellae are transmitted by the faecal-oral route. Infection produces an acute enterocolitis and fever with possible secondary complications such as septicaemia.

Prevention: Use of protective clothing, personal hygiene which include hand washing after contact with animals or their waste, and sanitation measures prevent the transmission of the disease.

Campylobacter: *Campylobacter* species can be found in pet and laboratory animal species. Transmission to humans is by the faecal-oral route and can produce an acute enteritis. Symptoms include diarrhoea, abdominal pain, fever, nausea, and vomiting.

Prevention: Use of protective clothing such as gloves, good personal hygiene, and sanitation measures will help to prevent the transmission of the disease.

APPENDIX 5 – FLUID CHART

Weight	Species (adults)		5%	7%	10%	Maintenance 5%	Max Amount at one time
			ml	ml	ml	ml	ml
10 g	Blue Tit Coal Tit	Long Tailed Tit Wren	0.5	0.7	1	0.5	0.1
20g	Great Tit Dunnock Robin Blackcap	Bullfinch Goldfinch Wagtail Housemartin	1	1.4	2	1	0.2
30g	Chaffinch Greenfinch	Sparrow	1.5	2.1	3	1.5	0.3
40g	Kingfisher		2	2.8	4	2	0.4
50g			2.5	3.5	5	2.5	0.5
60g			3	4.2	6	3	0.6
70g			3.5	4.9	7	3.5	0.7
80g			4	5.6	8	4	0.8
90g			4.5	6.3	9	4.5	0.9
100g	Blackbird Great Spotted Woodpecker	Starling Thrush	5	7	10	5	1
200g	Collared Dove Green Woodpecker Jackdaw	Kestrel Little Owl Magpie Sparrowhawk	10	14	20	10	2
300g	Barn Owl Black Headed Gull Feral Pigeon	Moorhen Woodcock	15	21	30	15	3
400g	Partridge Rook	Wood Pigeon	20	28	40	20	4
500g	Carrion Crow Tawny Owl		25	35	50	25	5
600g			30	42	60	30	6
700g			35	49	70	35	7
800g	Coot		40	56	80	40	8
900g	Lesser Black Back Gull		45	63	90	45	9
1000g	Buzzard Herring Gull Red Kite		50	70	100	50	10
1500g	Heron Mallard Pheasant		75	105	150	55	15
2000g	Cormorant		100	140	200	60	20
4000g	Canada Goose		200	280	400	65	40

Calc for fluid replacements:- Dehydration% (5% mild – 10% severe) + Maintenance amount = Fluid Replacement Required over 24 hours.

Do not exceed the max amount shown per time

APPENDIX 6 – IDENTIFICATION CHART

Insect Eaters

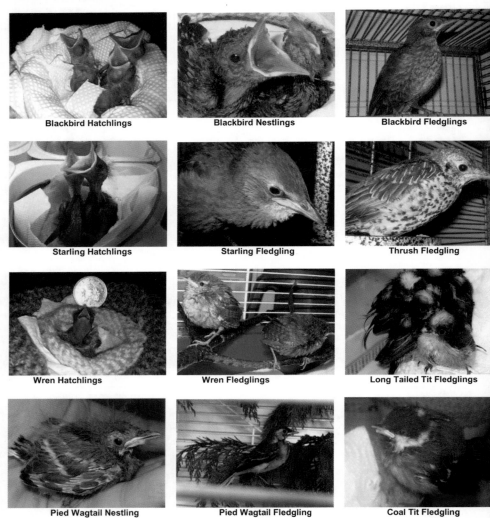

Blackbird Hatchlings   Blackbird Nestlings   Blackbird Fledglings

Starling Hatchlings   Starling Fledgling   Thrush Fledgling

Wren Hatchlings   Wren Fledglings   Long Tailed Tit Fledglings

Pied Wagtail Nestling   Pied Wagtail Fledgling   Coal Tit Fledgling

Insect Eaters

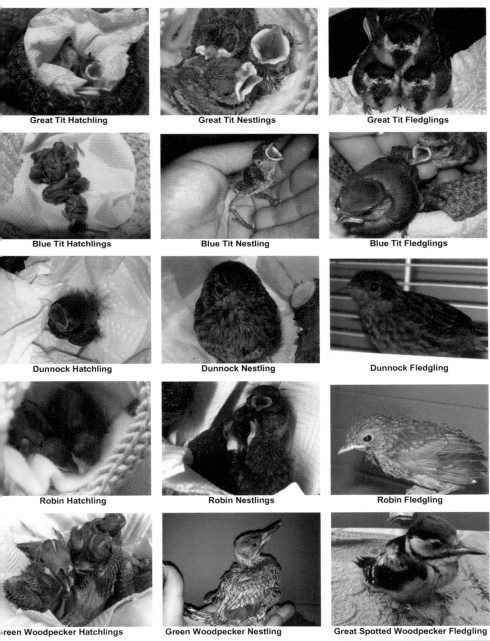

Great Tit Hatchling	Great Tit Nestlings	Great Tit Fledglings
Blue Tit Hatchlings	Blue Tit Nestling	Blue Tit Fledglings
Dunnock Hatchling	Dunnock Nestling	Dunnock Fledgling
Robin Hatchling	Robin Nestlings	Robin Fledgling
Green Woodpecker Hatchlings	Green Woodpecker Nestling	Great Spotted Woodpecker Fledgling

Seed Eaters

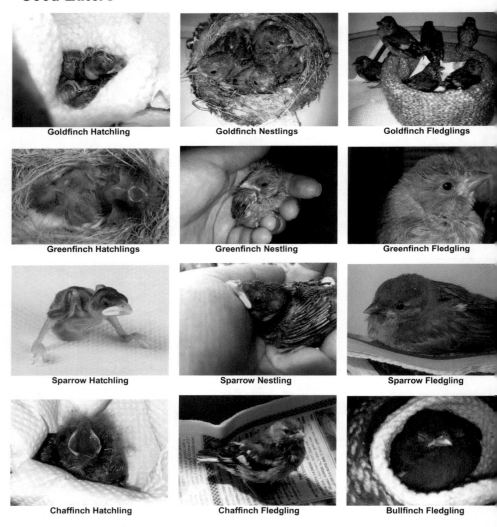

Goldfinch Hatchling   Goldfinch Nestlings   Goldfinch Fledglings

Greenfinch Hatchlings   Greenfinch Nestling   Greenfinch Fledgling

Sparrow Hatchling   Sparrow Nestling   Sparrow Fledgling

Chaffinch Hatchling   Chaffinch Fledgling   Bullfinch Fledgling

Corvids

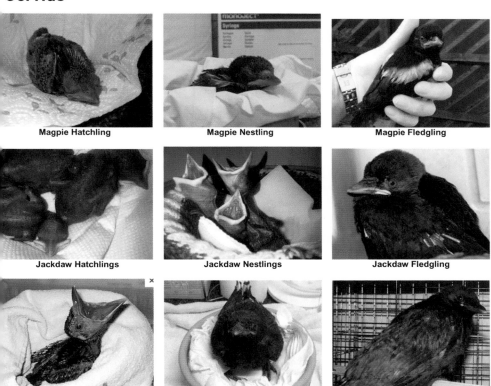

Magpie Hatchling | Magpie Nestling | Magpie Fledgling

Jackdaw Hatchlings | Jackdaw Nestlings | Jackdaw Fledgling

Crow Hatchling | Crow Nestling | Crow Fledgling

Birds Of Prey

Barn Owl Nestling	Barn Owl Chick	Barn Owl Fledgling
Tawny Owl Hatchling	Tawny Owl Chick	Barn Owl Fledgling
Little Owl Chick	Little Owl Chick	Little Owl Fledgling
Kestrel Chicks	Kestrel Chicks	Kestrel Fledgling

Pigeons & Doves

Collared Dove Hatchling

Collared Dove Nestling

Collared Dove Fledglings

Wood Pigeon Hatchling

Wood Pigeon Nestling

Wood Pigeon Fledgling

Stock Dove Nestling

Stock Dove Nestling

Stock Dove Fledgling

Feral Pigeon Hatchling

Feral Pigeon Nestling

Feral Pigeon Fledgling

Hirundines

House Martin Nestling

House Martin Fledgling

Swallow Fledgling

Swift Nestling

Swift Chick

Game Birds

Pheasant Chick

Pheasant Chick

Partridge Chick

Water Birds

Gosling

Cygnet

Cygnet

Coot Chick

Moorhen Chick

Moorhen Juvenile

Mallard Duckling

Shelduck Duckling

Tufted Duckling

Lapwing Chick

Lapwing Chick

Gull Chicks

INDEX

3231601R10043

Printed in Great Britain
by Amazon.co.uk, Ltd.,
Marston Gate.